Navigating Your

Journey

Navigating Your Journey

Actionable Leadership Lessons

for Women Who
Want to Have It ALL

VICKI UPDIKE

Advantage.

Published by Advantage, Charleston, South Carolina.
Member of Advantage Media Group.

ADVANTAGE is a registered trademark, and the Advantage colophon is a trademark of Advantage Media Group, Inc.

Printed in the United States of America.

10 9 8 7 6 5 4 3 2 1

ISBN: 978-1-64225-279-8
LCCN: 2021917526

Book design by Mary Hamilton.

This publication is designed to provide accurate and authoritative information in regard to the subject matter covered. It is sold with the understanding that the publisher is not engaged in rendering legal, accounting, or other professional services. If legal advice or other expert assistance is required, the services of a competent professional person should be sought.

Advantage Media Group is proud to be a part of the Tree Neutral® program. Tree Neutral offsets the number of trees consumed in the production and printing of this book by taking proactive steps such as planting trees in direct proportion to the number of trees used to print books. To learn more about Tree Neutral, please visit **www.treeneutral.com**.

Advantage Media Group is a publisher of business, self-improvement, and professional development books and online learning. We help entrepreneurs, business leaders, and professionals share their Stories, Passion, and Knowledge to help others Learn & Grow. Do you have a manuscript or book idea that you would like us to consider for publishing? Please visit **advantagefamily.com**.

To Brendan and Lucy, who give me courage, motivation,
and so much joy on my journey.

CONTENTS

ACKNOWLEDGMENTS

I want to first give my deepest gratitude to my husband Jim. Without his encouragement and confidence in me, I would never have had the courage to go out on my own and start my business. This book would never have happened. He is the force behind the scenes for me, always there when I get stuck, asking, "Vicki, what would you tell your clients to do?" He is the coach to the coach.

Jim, every day you give me the strength I need to continue. Thank you. Love you.

I come from a really close family, which has been so incredibly meaningful for me in my journey. I even moved back to northeast Wisconsin so that my children would be raised with their cousins, aunts, uncles, and grandparents. My parents gave me the foundation that set me on this trajectory. They are still an active part of my life and continue to be the amazing parents they always were.

Mom and Dad, thank you for always instilling value in me.

And finally, I want to thank all of the teammates, coworkers, managers, bosses, leaders, and other colleagues I have associated with in my professional life. My gratitude for everyone would fill an entire book. Each person has taught me something and played a role in helping me grow.

Thank you for being a part of my journey.

INTRODUCTION

This book is a part of my journey. I didn't write it to define what it means to "have it all." I'm not the expert in that. I'm not saying you have to be the president of a company or even an executive. But I *am* saying that "having it all" is a very satisfying goal and one you deserve. For me, one of the components of having it all was that I needed financial stability to raise my two young kids. I never wanted them to worry. I was a single mom, and I needed to find a way to be financially independent. It also included being fulfilled in the work I was doing. That was my "all."

Many years ago, I was as far away from having it all as I could get, but I didn't know that until I had a sudden revelation. It happened in a department meeting when our vice president came in and half sat on the table. That was typical. He never stayed long. Ever. Instead, he started in on some dumb joke about a Shania Twain song.

I sat there in the back of the room, shaking my head slightly as I watched all the people around me nod and smile. *Oh, how charming! Isn't that funny?* But we all knew it wasn't funny. It was a waste of our time and did nothing for us as a team. It was all about his ego and nothing more.

I looked around and wondered if anyone even knew that I was there. It was at that moment that I had a moment of sudden insight. I didn't belong there. And I didn't want to!

I knew I had more to give than just nodding and smiling. In this room, there was nobody I could lean on. Nobody to tell me I was needed, that I had value, and that my job mattered. I didn't know where the company was going. And I definitely didn't know my role in getting the company there. I hadn't ever heard the president talk in the three years I was there. I felt helpless and useless and invisible as these executives walked around like they owned the world, but they didn't even know my name.

Something needed to change.

I had tried to conform and tried to play the game. I remember going up the elevator to work in the morning and the people in the elevator wouldn't even say good morning to each other. I felt lost and dismissed. My prevailing thought for the rest of the meeting was "I have to get out of here."

As soon as it was over, I went straight to my office and opened a job search engine. Within moments, a leadership position popped up closer to my hometown. Even though I was pretty doubtful I was at all qualified for it, I applied and landed an interview.

A few days later, I drove the three hours to interview in my blue minivan, blasting Bon Jovi's "It's My Life." As I pulled into the parking lot, I looked in the rearview mirror and said to myself, "Let's do this."

I walked into that interview ready to take on the world, knowing I was going to land this job. And I did. This book is going to tell you to take on the world, even in those moments when you feel so full of self-doubt that you can't even look up from your shoes. I don't want anybody to have that helpless feeling and think that they have to stay in that.

You can take control of your career. You navigate your journey. I know because I was all alone in that pit. I was definitely an invisible member of a team. I didn't know my value. But after many years and a whole lot of mistakes, I took control of my journey.

This book contains the lessons I have learned on the leadership journey that took place before and after I was in that very low moment. Along the way, I have realized that leadership is never a destination. It is truly a journey. Even though I was president, I'm still not done. I thought I was going to be in corporate America forever. I never saw myself as an entrepreneur, and yet here I am now, running my own company. I have so much more I want to do. I always like to see myself in my next role.

Everyone has challenges in their career. There are times when you definitely feel like you're stepping backward. There are times when you're stuck. Leadership can be a lonely place sometimes, and not every place is a perfect fit. Those challenges don't go away. I hear women today who are dealing with the same things. I don't want you to feel alone.

Your journey is completely personal, which means it can only be defined by YOU. No one else can define it for you. Not society. Not a husband or partner. Not friends. Not the media or your networks. Not a boss. Your journey will look drastically different from everyone else's.

At the heart of this book is a simple premise: there is great power in knowing your value. And only you are in control. You can continue to move forward because you're not done either. You can do it all, and you can have it all, whatever "it all" means for you. You can do it. It's obtainable, and it happens faster than you think.

CHAPTER ONE

The Journey from Doer to Leader

"**S**o how does it feel to be a woman president?"

Hearing this earnest question from the reporter from our local newspaper, I tried not to laugh.

"I'm not sure what you want me to say. I've always been a woman. And I'm a president. What does one have to do with the other?"

Unsurprisingly, that quote never made it into the article, but to this day, I shake my head at the silliness of it all.

Throughout my leadership journey, I have experienced many of the same bumps and roadblocks we all face as we go from individual contributor to business leader. I have been lower than low. Some would say I have risen to the top. And I think it's fair to say I made many mistakes along the way. Even today, I am learning and challenging myself.

The notion of "having it all" changes over time and from person to person. This book is written out of a desire for you to realize you can have it all, whatever "all" means to you.

My "all" has changed during my career. I started out simply wanting to have a career that made a difference. Then it shifted to wanting to have a greater influence on results and strategy. The meaning of having it "all" continued to morph as I had kids, went through a divorce, spent time as a single mother, and experienced other life changes. My "all," at one point, meant simply being able to financially support myself and my kids. Then, as I continued on my leadership journey and my children grew, it shifted yet again.

Of course, my definition of "all" is not yours, nor should it be. But I want you to know you CAN have it all on your own terms. In the end, it is a wonderful feeling to strive at the place where I am comfortable saying I have it all. Every woman deserves the same!

In this book, I offer suggestions and tips to help you on your journey of having it all. I'm compelled to share my leadership journey filled with successes and failures and the lessons I've learned on the way. There is no reason you have to have the same heartache and struggles. The wisest people are those who learn from others' mistakes. Well, here are a whole lot of my mistakes. I hope that you can learn from them and save time on your journey to live your "all."

See Who You Want to Be

I was a doer. From the very start of my career, I enjoyed being the person others could depend on to find the answers to challenging questions. I got shit done. But it turned out this characteristic ended up developing into a defining factor in my career and eventually led to my greatest leadership challenges.

But more on that later.

As an eager twenty-two-year-old, I wanted to put my shiny new business diploma to work. I didn't know if there were even jobs out there for people like me, but like everyone in those days, I opened up the newspaper and turned to the want ads to find out.

I was excited and a bit relieved when I found an entry-level position at a company where I could actually use my education.

For the next three years, I associated with some of the best businesspeople in the industry. Of course, I couldn't have known the sheer luck I had of starting in an environment where every voice was valued and everyone who worked there was a part of a team.

I remember expecting classic corporate USA. I assumed the leaders were a mysterious thing in a separate wing with glass-walled offices filled with beautiful things. I assumed I would have my little square of the world, and I would do whatever my little square of the world was supposed to do.

But that wasn't the case. It was shockingly inclusive. But I didn't know exactly how special that was, that it was an anomaly in the business world—especially at that time. From the very start, I associated with people outside my department, from vice presidents all the way down to the little doers like me. I was shown where I fit in the bigger picture. I truly understood how my work had an impact on the greater goals of the company.

I was shocked at how much work it was, though. It's fair to say that the work was hard, as we were all committed to the success of the company. It grew astronomically over the period of time when I happened to be there. But it worked because we knew each other, we trusted each other, and we talked to each other. Leaders shared the real thing. They didn't just tell you what you wanted to hear or just the component that they thought you needed to know. It was a great place to be.

It was here, at this very early stage in my career, where I began my leadership journey. I didn't really know exactly what I wanted to do in my career or exactly who I wanted to be, but I was very aware of what was going on around me. There were two women I looked up to and used as my role models, my manager and the vice president of my department.

Even today, I still think of them as my mentors. They couldn't have known how influential they were to me, but they set me on my path. They had no idea how much I looked up to them and how much I was learning from them.

My manager had a real authenticity about her, and I loved that. She brought trust to everyone she worked with. She had an executive meeting once a month and invited me to join because I helped her create the data behind it. I was so proud of my little role!

The goal of these important meetings was to forecast sales. I remember watching in awe as all of the executives listened so intently to her presentations. I thought, *I want to do that!* I saw in her the leader I wanted to be, and I paid attention to what that meant. She held the room with so much calmness, respect, and trust. I knew I wanted to have those moments where my participation was meaningful. I saw my next step in my leadership journey.

She wasn't that much older than me, but she had an executive presence. This was my first lesson. About a year later, I was put in that position. I was now the one explaining the numbers and answering questions for major decisions. I learned through this experience that it really doesn't matter what your position or title is. It was about your ability to contribute, and I liked that. I thrived on that.

The other role model I had at the time was the vice president of marketing. She could captivate a room. She was so stinking smart, and her skills were amazing. She knew exactly what she was doing. She walked and talked and dressed like a leader. On the outside, she looked the part. Business suits, nice accessories, everything you'd expect but with no pretention. She carried around a plain notepad where she would take notes. She wasn't about the image.

She always presented herself in a calm and thoughtful manner. Even when the day was crazy, that thoughtful demeanor instilled confidence and hope in us. But she didn't offer platitudes. With her, there was no sugarcoating, which immediately got the trust of the team around her.

I remember one particular meeting with the full marketing team. I caught a glimpse of the paper she had brought with her, expecting to see an agenda. I was wrong. She had only prepared a few notes written in pencil, just bullet points with a few words to guide the conversation. The rest of the meeting she wanted to know how we were doing and what we needed to achieve our goals. She wanted to hear from us instead of telling us what to do.

She moved up to be the president of that company. For someone to move from vice president of marketing to company-wide president is a rare move—maybe 15 percent or less—but she did it. And I did it!

To this day, I've never shared with these two women the impact that they had on my career, but I go back to what they taught me. Granted, I got lost for a while when I left that company. I didn't find the same atmosphere in my next job, but I couldn't have known that when I moved.

Take the Good Stuff, Shed the Negative

I was presented a new opportunity at a new company closer to home and with a sizable raise. At this point in my life, I knew that money wasn't the best goal, but for an eager young professional, it was hard to pass up. I took the opportunity and began the next chapter of my leadership journey.

When I went to the manager of my old job to turn in my resignation and explained my reasons, I insisted that I would be content in this new job. He said, "Oh no, Vicki. You're not done. You're going to run a company someday."

He saw in me the desire to continue to have influence and impact others. I thought he was nuts. I had young kids at home. How could I do more?

Changing jobs is hard. It always takes a while to acclimate and to figure out where you fit in a new place. After the warm and nurturing environment I had been in, I wasn't ready for what I found. I didn't know how to react when I discovered that my opinions weren't valued. In team meetings, there was very little interaction and conversation. The manager would say a few things to the people there, and that was it. There was no culture of learning from each other or working together.

It was the type of environment where everybody worked in their own cubicles with little authentic communication or relationships of substance. I felt scripted. I had to be something I knew I wasn't in order to fit in. And I still didn't fit in.

I wasn't in the group of people who had been there for twenty years. I was that new person, the outsider, and I was not included.

We all did what we did. And that was it. There was no shared vision. I rarely heard from any member of the executive team in the four years I was there. These men were in meetings, doing things behind closed doors. I didn't know them, and they certainly didn't know me. Comparing my first environment to this one, I didn't know which was the "real" business environment. But I knew what I wanted.

To survive, I had to tell myself, "This is how the business world works." So I just did the task at hand.

Until the day when I just couldn't take it anymore. I realized that I didn't want a career there, and I certainly didn't want to be a leader in that environment. Sometimes we have to go through those moments to learn that it's OK to walk away.

This is where I was able to learn my next lesson. I knew the leadership skills I wanted to use in my next role, and I knew this wasn't the right environment.

I had to learn to let go of those things that did not represent me. I was not someone who sat behind closed doors and had conversations that excluded others. I didn't love that job, but I am grateful for it because it taught me so much. That place gave me another lens of leadership. I took the good and tried to shed the negative.

Knowing what you don't want is as important as knowing and seeing what you do want

Knowing what you *don't* want is as important as knowing and seeing what you *do* want. This gave me the experience to see the leadership behaviors I didn't want. I wouldn't be the leader I am today without seeing that.

The Move from Doer to Leader

In my next company, I was hired as a marketing manager, and I still got shit done. I was very proud of that. My value and influence continued to grow. I liked to be the person who others could come to for the answers. But I didn't realize that I was bulldozing my way. Because I just wanted to be smart and have the answers, I wasn't building the right relationships. I learned the hard way that this attitude can only get you so far.

I was having a positive impact on business results but also giving off the vibe for everyone to get out of my way. I believed I was being efficient and effective, but really I was telling people what to do. That's not the leader or team member I needed to be. I know now that I was being oblivious to the impact of my actions. People didn't trust me because of how self-centered I was.

To snap me out of that, I had a humbling experience when I was a relatively new executive. The lesson haunts me to this day.

I was in a meeting with the rest of the executive team and it became clear that we were having some IT issues. Feeling it was my responsibility as the new VP of marketing to make a contribution, I challenged the man who was over the IT department. In front of all the other executives, I confidently folded my arms, looked him in the eye, and asked, "What are you doing to solve these problems?"

Looking back on this, I am so embarrassed! I can't believe I'm even sharing this story! Here I was, a young new executive on the team, putting this very seasoned vice-president on the spot in front of the rest of the executives. He was probably a good twenty years older than me. What gave me the right to demand that he solve the problem alone? You'd think after all I learned in my first job that I would know better.

But no, instead of being a team player, I drove a wedge. My message to him was "You (and you alone) need to get it done."

Unsurprisingly, he was pretty bothered. The day after that meeting, he walked into my office and closed the door. He calmly told me that the way I treated him was inappropriate and that he didn't sleep well that night. It left me speechless.

Think about the depth of character it took for him to quietly bring this to my attention outside of the team meeting rather than just blowing me off or worse, humiliating me in return. He was dedicated enough to the success of the team to have a very uncomfortable conversation with the sole purpose of helping me be better.

And it worked. I realized the impact of my attitude on everyone around me. If he fails, I fail. *We* fail. If my team fails, I fail. We all fail. We were all connected. From that conversation on, building trust became so much more important.

I am comforted at the thought that if I were to have that conversation today, it would be much different. I was young and aggressive and driven to prove myself as an executive. Up until that point, I hadn't done the self-reflection to think about how I could be better as a leader vs. the doer in me.

When I put the mirror up to myself, I realized that people didn't trust me. I was self-centered on what I alone thought we needed to get done, so I had to learn this important leadership lesson. Trust is the foundation.

As my career moved forward, I found that, even with my newfound revelation about the importance of teamwork, I continued to stumble. Old habits die hard.

In another executive meeting years later, I presented the development of a new product. In order for my idea to happen, I told the vice president of operations that he had to make some production changes in manufacturing.

He looked across the table at me and calmly said, "No."

My old self would have challenged him immediately and demanded compliance with my request. This time, though, I was smart enough to hold my tongue. After the meeting was over, I went into my office and wrote my thoughts down. Then I nervously set up a private meeting with him.

That was a very humbling moment. I realized, again, that success depends on cooperation between all involved. It's not just about what I wanted to do.

In our meeting, he just sat there, not saying anything while I read off all the reasons he should support me. Then I waited, anxiously fidgeting with my keys. Here is this wonderfully smart executive just listening, and I am very aware that he doesn't have to lift a finger to help me.

There was a bottle opener on my keychain that I kept playing with to keep my hands busy. His eyes went to it, and then, instead of addressing anything I had just said, he pointed.

"Vicki, is that a church key?"

That's what some people jokingly call a bottle opener on a key chain. Completely taken off guard, I stammered some sort of confirmation.

Then he said, "I haven't seen that in a while."

And with that, a smile broke across his face and we talked about getting the project done. From that point, we worked on our product idea together, and it was successfully launched.

He knew how hard it was for me to come humbly seeking his help, and he didn't take advantage of that. He met me where I was, brought a lightness to the situation, and showed me how a team really could (and should!) function. We worked together for many years after that, and I respect him deeply to this day.

After many years and a lot of practice, I was finally able to let go of the "doer" attitude and be a true leader. My responsibilities and influence continued to grow at that company. I learned that being a leader isn't about being the only one to have the answers.

Rather, leadership is about having questions and creating the environment for your team to collectively find answers.

I eventually was promoted into the president's role. It's funny how, as I moved through my leadership journey, I DID less and less but CREATED so much more, creating a culture with a team of leaders and doers that are so much better than me and my single contribution.

Leadership is about having questions and creating the environment for your team to collectively find answers.

Being a president was about holding up the doers and watching them flourish. It wasn't about my specific tasks of the day. It was all about the team around me. Collaborating, inspiring, and encouraging became my tasks at hand as a leader—so much different than the technical tasks of an eager young marketing analyst.

Having It ALL:
Actionable Leadership Lessons

You've probably figured out by now that your sense of self is where this journey begins, knowing who you are today and who you want to become.

To continue your leadership journey, you can't be a passive observer. You need to take purposeful action. Below, and at the end of every chapter, you will find specific, actionable steps you can take today to move along in that purposeful way. You got this, and I believe in you.

Suggested Actions:

- Remember, you (and only you) get to define what "it all" means. Spend some quiet time today defining what your "all" is.

- See your next step. Consider what "it all" will mean in the future. Write down two next steps to get you there. Write down a few big steps that you will need to take to get to the ultimate "all."

- Reflect on the attributes of the leaders you truly admire. What are the traits you'd like to emulate? Reflect on the attributes of those less effective leaders around you. What is it you don't want?

Download the free journaling worksheets or purchase the reflection guide workbook at **www.vickiupdike.com/ navigatingyourjourney**.

CHAPTER TWO

Knowing Your Value

I had a unique relationship with a woman who had previously been a coworker and then later became one of my coaching clients, so I knew her on different levels. She rose to a leadership position in her company, which didn't surprise me because she was so dang smart. But she had a habit of undervaluing herself. Her self-doubt was causing her to deflate her value, and as a result, she would always downplay her contributions.

She saw her work as a list of tasks instead of truly understanding what the tasks resulted in. In her mind, she just was doing a lot of things. But in reality, those things added so much more to her workplace and her value; she just didn't see it or identify with it.

She is a high performing doer. But the doer in her couldn't see that her collective knowledge was so much greater than the list of tasks. We worked together to allow her to see herself as a leader. In our conversations, I would tell her, "I wish you could see what I see." This is so common; we downplay our value and have a hard time understanding when others see more in us.

We worked through her value proposition, and it wasn't long before she was able to start articulating her value. She had to step back and reflect on the impact and outcomes of all the tasks. She realized that others valued her contributions way more than the tasks she was competent in performing. Once she understood how people relied on her, her perspective changed. She was able to see that what may have seemed to be a minor task to her before was truly a very important component of what she did at work.

She had to start understanding her value as a leader.

Finding Your Value

It is important for women to know their value. I feel that, on the whole, we women downplay our value. The way we define our worth (also called our value proposition) is our own to define. Your value proposition encompasses the important aspects of who you are.

Our value doesn't come from the department we work in, the title we have, or the company that sends us a paycheck

Our value doesn't come from the department we work in, the title we have, or the company that sends us a paycheck. That's not where the value lies.

Do you think you'd be more valuable with a vice president's title or even a president's title? No. Your value is in what you contribute, in what you bring to your place of work in a way that is unique to you.

So often we fall back on the tasks we do to derive meaning and importance, but you are more than that. Your value proposition is based on outcomes and results, not tasks and titles. You may be surprised how often value is different than a job title. Instead of linking your value to your job description, think about what you bring to the role you happen to be in right now.

If you're struggling to find or understand your value, think about how others depend on you.

Try to answer questions such as:

- What do I do well, and who does it best serve?

- What are the specific contributions I make to my team?

- What does my team look for me to do?

- What do they depend on me for?

- What, specifically, do I bring to the table that nobody else does?

In one of my early jobs, my title was marketing analyst, which meant I was ultimately responsible for sales. But when I look back at that time, I think my real contribution was that I was able to sift through data, notice trends, and identify opportunities. Although I sat in marketing with a marketing title, my value went beyond that. I provided a unique ability to answer challenging questions. I could have had a dozen different titles in different departments or even different companies and still been able to provide the same value.

We, as women, don't spend enough time thinking and working on this. We downplay the impact we have on others around us. Don't diminish the credit you deserve for your accomplishments and your impact. That does nothing for you, and it's not necessary.

Be bold, not bashful. Be you! There are components of you that are purely you. We are all quirky and unique, and that is wonderful. Embrace it.

Don't diminish the credit you deserve for your accomplishments and your impact. That does nothing for you, and it's not necessary.

You may have some eye-opening revelations about things you take for granted. I remember a brief experience from another job that showed me that my value to my boss was broader than I realized. He was president, and I was vice president.

He was of a generation raised without much technology and, as a result, was not very comfortable with certain computer programs. We were sitting together on a flight going over an important PowerPoint for a joint presentation to be given shortly after we landed. As we went through it, we found places where it needed to be tweaked. He was trying to keep track of all the changes so he could have his assistant make the changes as soon as we touched down.

Smiling, I just grabbed the computer and went into the presentation and made the changes directly. He was impressed that we could actually update the file ourselves. I just looked at him and said, "We got this."

After a little while, we knew we had a better presentation. That was the value I brought. We were able to create a better presentation. It went beyond just the ability to know PowerPoint.

We all know how easy it is to make a PowerPoint presentation, but to him it was a highly valuable skill.

In that moment, I had a choice to either blow off his gratitude and praise, telling him it wasn't a big deal, or I could allow my value to be appreciated for what it was—a skill that was needed at the time. My skill was crucial because it improved our presentation. I did something we needed. While PowerPoint wasn't really part of my value proposition, the outcome was.

If I would have said, "Oh, it was nothing," that would've just diminished that confidence he had in me and would have limited my value proposition. What I did do was go beyond the task I had performed and looked at the impact I was having. He was right. His assistant could have made the changes. But by changing the document in real time while the two of us were discussing it created a better understanding, resulting in a great meeting.

It's funny. I look at my career now and realize I'm not so different from him in certain respects. For example, I know nothing about updating my website. Website development is a complete mystery to me, so what may seem so simple to others is so valuable to me. I truly depend on someone else to do it, not because it is complex, necessarily, but simply because I value it.

Clarifying Your Value

I remember giving my first presentation. There were probably twenty people meeting in a small conference room. It was a meaningful group, and I needed to communicate some important data. This may date me a little bit, but it's fun to look back in time. I had three very simple trend line graphs—you know, the X and Y axis with data plotted on the grid.

I got up there, feeling pretty nervous, but I just took a breath and started delivering what I had rehearsed, talking about what those lines were telling us. I was the one interpreting this complex information on that simple little line chart, and as I went along, I noticed people were listening to me. They were nodding their heads; they understood. I knew in that moment that I loved presenting. The anxiety I had going in was replaced with pride. It was a good moment. And even though that happened a long time ago, it was one of the foundational experiences of my career. I added value by presenting information for everyone to understand.

That ambitious young woman sitting there with her data is still a part of me even today. Many years later, I established a women's leadership conference that hundreds of people come to. Every year, I have the opportunity to stand in the back of the conference hall, listening to brilliant speakers on the stage. Looking at the women in the audience, they are listening and are engaged. That young woman at the overhead projector went on to create a space for other women to reflect, learn, and grow together. I don't have to have an overhead projector anymore, but I am still finding ways of sharing information with others who seek it.

I'm guessing you will have, and maybe even have already had, some of those moments as well where you have a sudden understanding of what you enjoy and what you're good at.

As you begin to consider your value, I challenge you to go further than simply stating, "I am good at Microsoft Word." Instead, think about the value or the outcome of knowing that program. I went from "I'm a marketing analyst" to "I know how to interpret data to get at complex business issues." Say you are an IT person. Rather than saying "I create code," you can say something like "I improve processes and systems." Reflect on what the tasks do. What are the outcomes you create?

There is merit in documenting your thoughts through this process as well. It can simply be bullet points, a phrase, a few sentences, whatever. I suggest you take some time to really think through and write down your value proposition. It is important because knowing your value leads to confidence and exuding that confidence.

If you don't know where to begin as you think about your value proposition, ask someone you trust who has worked with you. If it feels awkward, just blame it on me. Go to them and say, "I'm reading this book and I have to ask someone this question. What do you depend on me for? What do I bring to the team?"

And then listen—really listen—to what they say. Believe it or not, this simple act can really help you see the difference between your intentions and your actual impact. What you may believe about yourself may not be reality. Most likely, it's so much more.

Let us go through an exercise I use with my clients to help them define their value.

PASSIONS AND BELIEFS

When I help women clarify their value, I like to place an emphasis on passions and beliefs first.

Let's start with passion. **Passion is an emotion to be acted upon.** It is a strong desire that can get you to do amazing things; it's determination, a conviction, a position. Passions can be hard to define but worth giving voice to. They can become a journey in itself. Don't get frustrated.

Try answering these questions:

- What inspires me to take action?

- What motivates me to speak up?

- What compels me to take risks?

- What excites me?

Another approach is to simply complete this sentence: "I am _____ ."

Again, I want you to be bold. Use powerful words.

When you fill in those blanks, own it. Embrace the passion you have. Do you notice how we move from job description to rooting out the core aspects in you that you have a heart for? Think about your personality and your preferences.

Everyone has nonnegotiables that drive our beliefs. **Beliefs are facts that you accept to be true, often without question.** I find that often these nonnegotiables are discovered during hard times. They are formed throughout our lives and are influenced by the positive and negative experiences we have. If you start to analyze what stresses you out, you'll likely start to realize what your nonnegotiables are. It's important for you to recognize these because you don't want to fight them. If you do, that will be a source of significant tension.

For me, when I was in work environments that didn't feel authentic, I struggled. I recognized this was a source of strain for me, which led me to learn that authenticity is one of my core beliefs. I am straightforward and tell it like it is, and I appreciate that belief in others.

Passion is an emotion to be acted upon.

Beliefs are facts that you accept to be true, often without question.

SKILLS

The next thing I encourage women to do as they work on their value proposition is to consider what skills they fall back on repeatedly. These are things you can naturally do, things that you are good at, or things that you continue to learn. Don't let modesty hold you back.

Take some time to think about this, but you should have four or five things you recognize you are good at. Again, be bold. As you think about your skills, try asking yourself questions like:

- What have I achieved?

- What am I good at?

- What am I especially proud of?

- What things do I use on a frequent basis?

In a professional setting, these are the dependencies. Maybe you're a graphic designer. Rather than saying "I am a graphic designer," you could say, "I create beautiful things using my computer skills." Or, if you're a technical writer, you could say, "I ensure accuracy in communication."

But don't forget those softer, more social skills. It might be presenting to large groups, being an active listener, or naturally taking the lead in difficult conversations.

Don't worry if these things are not super unique. To get to a certain point in our careers, there are certain abilities we all master, and that's a good thing. But I urge you to be realistic and bold. Create this self-awareness; it's a good thing.

EXPERIENCES

Finally, think about the experiences you have had that continue to move you forward. This is what really makes you *you*. Nobody else on the planet can bring the perspective you bring because nobody has had the exact same set of experiences, good and bad.

What are the unique experiences that have shaped you, especially in your career, both positive and negative? It could be influences from a culture where you worked. It could be about an opportunity that you were given. It could be a promotion that came or didn't come.

For me, one of my most impactful experiences goes back to the story I shared in the previous chapter at my first job. I saw someone I admired doing something I wanted to do. I wanted to be that leader. That unique experience was formative for me in that I was able to recognize what I admired and what I wanted to be like. Later on, I had a very negative experience in a job that was extremely siloed, and as a result, I do not want to be seen as a silo driver. These experiences are still a component of my value proposition.

Reflect on your passions, your skills, and your experiences. As you pull all that together in your value statement, you will also have more clarity on what you need for the next step, goal setting.

Establishing Your Goals

Once you better understand your value, the next natural step is to think about how you want to use your value. Early in my career, I didn't establish goals on my career journey. Honestly, I didn't even recognize I was even on a journey or that there was a next step.

Whether you recognize it or not, you are also on a journey, so I suggest you make it an intentional one. As the old saying goes, if you don't know where you're going, how will you know when you get there? Where do you want to go?

The way to be intentional about your journey is to set goals. I'm not talking about business goals. We all have those, and they are fine, but I'm talking about personal development goals. It may be "I want to speak up at the next meeting," "I will accept the next hard assignment that comes along," or "I want to be the president of this company one day." If you're not sure where you want to go, reflect on your passions, beliefs, and skills. How do you want to use your value?

There were times I thought I was giving all that I had, but I felt like every contribution I offered was ignored or fell on deaf ears. You probably have felt that at some point too. Maybe you are feeling that way today. I get it. I understand, but you are the driver of your professional journey. This journey you are on doesn't happen *to* you. It happens *because* of you. It is important to recognize that you are the control factor.

To put it another way, *you* are entirely up to *you*.

There are always options in front of us, but I have watched an unfortunate pattern play out again and again when it comes to seeing those options. Women cut themselves short by preempting their choices. We too often take ourselves out of a choice before it is even presented. I hear things like "Oh, I could never be a manager" when the opportunity to be a manager hasn't even presented itself yet. Don't unintentionally hold *yourself* back.

Create bold goals. Don't create goals based on limiting beliefs. And don't make decisions toward those goals that aren't yours to make yet. You don't *need* to make a decision until you *have* to make a decision. Creating and having options is always a good thing because things change over time.

With that said, when a new opportunity does come along, go for it. Don't be afraid; do it anyway, particularly if it is something you think will be tough. If you don't think you're ready for something, that's OK. You will learn as you go. Do it anyway. Dive in headlong and trust that you'll figure it out. You never know how far you can go until you try.

When I was a vice president, I knew that I needed to complete my MBA to be considered for other promotions. And I really wanted those promotions. But I hated the thought of going back to school. I was in the middle of going through a divorce, had been promoted to VP, my kids were five and eight years old, and I felt like I was fully consumed. I flat out did not want to go back to school.

But I knew where I wanted to go in my career, and that was the only way. So, reluctantly, I signed up and started classes.

As a huge surprise to me, I loved it. I learned so much. I met great people. And it was because I took control of my journey. It took me longer than I had hoped, but we women are a resilient group. We figure things out. I knew my most productive time was in my office at night or early in the morning before the kids were up. I just made it work.

I remember my mom saying, "Vicki, you're going to look back at this and wonder how you did it all." And she was right! Looking back, it was a crazy, busy time, and I did it. Tackling that single goal brought me so much.

I also learned an important lesson—make a lifetime habit of setting goals for yourself. At one point when I was company president, I was giving a presentation about goal setting to a group of people. When I was finished, a young man came up to me and asked me, "So, Vicki, what's next for you?"

I was speechless. I hadn't realized I was so fully engaged in being a president that I had forgotten to keep setting goals for my professional development. That simple question set me back on the path of reflection. I was at another pivotal moment in my career. This was no time to stop learning and growing.

I want you to take everything you've learned and figure out what you need to be your best version of you. No one else can define your "best" version of yourself. Not me. Not society. Not a spouse or a partner. Not a boss.

Start with this: spend ten minutes today on your goals. You don't have to look too far out, just the next six months or year. Think about what motivates you. What brings you a sense of accomplishment? Where do you want to use your value?

Maybe you are currently working on a very complex project and you're excited about it. You want to finish this project and you want to do it well because it's giving you an opportunity to show your skills, to show your value. Set a goal to perform at your best during that project and show your value.

Maybe your goal is that you want to get a promotion in a year. That is a very good goal. But I then ask that you drill down a little bit further and come up with some subgoals because a promotion is a bold goal. What's the work you have to do to get a promotion? Outline that out.

If you don't know what the subgoals should be, I suggest you be brave and ask your boss what would make you promotable. You can ask something like "How do I move to the next level?"

Then listen and take notes on what they say. As I said before, don't worry if you don't feel ready or you don't feel like you're 100 percent. Good goals are going to be a stretch. Do it anyway. And remember, you're not alone. You have a network, which leads us to building relationships.

Building Your Relationships

Your network is so important!

I know. We all have a love-hate relationship with "networking." But all this word really means is building relationships with those around you, both inside and outside your organization. We often focus so much energy in building the network outside our organization that we overlook the importance of the network inside our company. But it's this internal network where you can best show your value.

One of the best examples I ever saw of building relationships at work was my coworker Alex. A weekly report would get distributed to key people in the company, and Alex always made a significant contribution to that report. After making his contribution each month, he took it a step further and used it to strengthen his network.

If he didn't know the people who used the report, he made a point to physically go through the office to find that person. Then he would spend some time getting to know them. He asked how and why they were using the report and how it could be more useful. He took the time to build the relationship with those who depended on him.

Eventually, it felt like he knew everybody in the company, and everybody knew him. He knew why people depended on him, even in very removed situations. He could talk to anyone. After seeing this happen, I stopped holding myself back. Watching him work his magic made me wonder why I ever hesitated to build relationships.

Build your network. Get to know the people you depend on or that depend on you to get the desired outcomes, even if you don't work with them directly. Ask yourself what you are doing to cultivate those relationships and what impact you have on them. The time when you need a network is not the time to be building a network.

There are going to be times when you can't get it all done by yourself, and you're going to need to know who to go to for help and how. And vice versa. There will be times when people will need you, and you will know how to be there for them.

This creates your tribe, those who best know you and the value you bring. These are the people you can lean on because they know your strengths, they understand your weaknesses, and you learn from each other.

As you grow in your career, your goals become bigger than just your individual skills. And the bigger the goals get, the less likely it is that you're going to be able to achieve them on your own. And when this happens, you, your real and authentic self, can lean on and depend on the network you created.

Early in my career, I thought I had to keep my work and my personal lives strictly separated. I even made sure to live in a different town so my two worlds wouldn't accidentally collide at the grocery store.

As I continued to learn and grow, I allowed myself to bring some of the authentic Vicki to the workplace. I was amazed to learn that once I started to put my guard down and be vulnerable, people started seeing me as a whole person rather than just the me that I was at work. I shared my family with my team. They saw how I cried when my son went to basic training. Those are the moments that made me *me*.

I also shared parts of my authentic self that brought me joy. I had to ignore my fear that they would judge me or laugh and just be open with them. I am a product of the '80s and have been a Bon Jovi fan all my life, which I really didn't share with the people I worked with. I felt it did not fit this "leader" persona I had in my head.

Well, one afternoon, it just came up. I was taking the afternoon off to travel to a Bon Jovi concert that evening. But rather than making a vague excuse like I had done in the past, I decided to risk embarrassment and just tell it like it is.

"I am going to Milwaukee for a Bon Jovi concert with my sisters."

It felt good that I could share my excitement with them. And they seemed to enjoy learning this about me. As I walked through the parking lot, one of them opened her window and started singing "Living on a Prayer" at me, loud and long. I just smiled and waved.

It felt so empowering that they knew me as a real person! (Although I didn't tell them it was my sixth concert that year!)

As women see, embrace, and enhance their value, it becomes harder to hide their true selves from those around them. Awareness of value leads to a greater sense of worth. And with greater self-worth comes a greater sense of confidence.

Having It ALL:
Actionable Leadership Lessons

As women understand their intrinsic value, they can't help but to rise. We rise above the muck and solve problems with perspective. It's amazing how quickly we can get bogged down in the minutia of life's problems when we forget who we really are. Your value does not depend on your title, your family, your social channels, or your appearance. You are valuable just because you are you. Never downplay that!

Remember, you are entirely up to you. Create bold goals that help you identify and use your value and then build your network inside and outside your organization. As you do this, you will continue to build trust with those around you.

Suggested Actions:

- Define and document your value. List your top five passions, beliefs, skills, and experiences that make you *you.*

- Clarify your professional value statement. What are the outcomes and results you create? Reflect back on the questions in this chapter.

- Create your top three professional development goals. Where are you going and how will you get there?

- Be you. List a few things that make you unique.

- Complete the sentence: I am _____

  _____!

Download the free journaling worksheets or purchase the reflection guide workbook at **www.vickiupdike.com/ navigatingyourjourney.**

CHAPTER THREE

Finding Confidence

According to a *Harvard Business Review* article, when comparing confidence ratings for men and women, there is a significant gap in those professionals under forty. A study concluded that it's highly probable that those women are far more competent than they think they are, while the male leaders are overconfident and assuming they are more competent than they are.[1]

This gap narrowed as the ages of surveyed businesspeople increased, and around age forty, confidence ratings merged.

What makes this even more interesting is that when managers were polled, women were rated higher than men in "virtually every functional area of the organization ... In fact, they were thought to

---

1   Zenger and Folkman, "Research: Women Score Higher Than Men in Most Leadership Skills," *Harvard Business Review*, June 25, 2019.

be more effective in 84 percent of the competencies that we most frequently measure."

Researchers found that women in their twenties and thirties are "less likely to apply for jobs unless they are confident they meet most of the qualifications. A man and a woman with identical credentials, who both lack experience for a higher-level position, come to different conclusions about being prepared for the promotion. The man is more inclined to assume that he can learn what he's missing while in the new job. He says to himself, "I am close enough." The woman is inclined to be more wary and less willing to step up in that circumstance."

What is upsetting about this fact is that women with similar levels of education and experience to their male counterparts will have a drastically different sense of their abilities. So the data suggests that you think you don't have enough competence as the guy sitting next to you when in reality you do. You just need to believe in yourself.

Confidence Is a Skill

I have found that while men seek coaching to up their actual skill, women tend to seek coaching to up their confidence. In fact, the number one thing I hear from women in my business is a lack of self-confidence, and this lack of self-confidence is holding them back.

I know that you're reading this book because you are a continuous learner. You wonder. You are curious. You find the answers you need. You look to continually build your skills.

Confidence is just another skill

Confidence is just another skill. And like all skills, you have to work on it before you achieve mastery. If you just sit back and wait to be confident, it will be a long wait. We are never 100 percent confident 100 percent of the time—it doesn't matter who you are or the title you may have. There are times when we perceive ourselves as not ready and therefore less confident than we need to be.

To be more confident is (and I know you'll roll your eyes at this) to just be more confident. I know how it sounds: have confidence by being confident. But try. You have to work through those less confident moments and continue forward regardless of the doubt, anxiety, fear, or whatever it is holding you back. It's in these moments where confidence is established and grows. You are building your confidence skill.

If you're thinking, *Sure, Vicki. Easier said than done*, I get it. There are always times that we feel we don't have the confidence we need. When I was a young executive presenting to others with way more experience than I did, I didn't even believe I was the one who should be there at all. It was nerve-racking, but I had to pull myself together. I know you know the technical components of your job. Now it's time to let others know. I didn't give myself a choice. I stood up and did it, and I didn't give myself the luxury of questioning if I could. It's in those moments where you are building confidence.

Every time you just do it, the ability to work through our less confident moments gets easier. Not that I ever felt I had all the confidence I needed to do every job I did. That's never going to happen. We always have that little bit of self-doubt, but we always have the choice to work through it.

Think of it this way. Nobody needs to see your confidence level. Confidence is inside of you. Others will never know you aren't as confident on the inside if you display confidence on the outside. This is not being fake or the unauthentic you. It is you building your confidence skill.

Midway through my career, I learned that I would actually begin to feel more confident inside when I showed confidence on the outside, especially when the stakes were high. As part of my job as president, I reported our performance to the board of directors. The environment in these meetings was very formal, and I felt a lot of pressure. I had to look and act the part. But yet, I was just Vicki from Green Bay. Mother, daughter, Packer fan. Yet in those moments, I was also competent and exuded the confidence of that competence.

After some years in this position, I slowly started to be my more authentic self. If I wanted to be the confident leader I had been envisioning all my career, I had to be true to who I really was.

One of the opportunities I had to do this was when we had not hit our goals as a company and I had to deliver news that I knew wouldn't be received well to people who had the authority to fire me. Rather than trying to mimic what others might do and soften the message with vague business speak, I chose to approach this in the way I was naturally inclined to approach all tough situations—head on.

I stood before this group and told them straight what went wrong and the impact that it had on performance. Then I addressed how we were going to fix it. I remembered the lessons from my vice president long ago, and I did not sugarcoat the message.

I was vulnerable, authentic, and exuded the confidence I felt I needed (but didn't necessarily feel), and the conversation I had with my board of directors that day reflected that. I talked to them like a partner, not a subordinate.

After the meeting, a board member came to me and said, "So, Vicki, have you always been like this?"

I took that as a compliment. "Yes, I have," I responded.

He said, "It's rather refreshing. Thank you for the clarity."

The director didn't need to know that I had self-doubt and had to work through my lack of confidence. I just responded, "Thank you." I had always had a true leader inside me. I just had to let her take the lead.

In that moment, I came full circle. I started my career knowing exactly what kind of leader I wanted to be. I struggled when I went to a place where there was no belonging. Upon leaving that environment, I lost sight of that leader. And now I had arrived at a place where I had proven to myself that I could truly add value by just being me. Even if I didn't have all the confidence all the time.

Pull Your Chair Up to the Table

You've probably heard this phrase before. It is common in the world of business, particularly among women leaders. Shirley Chisholm, the first African American woman elected to Congress and Sheryl Sandberg, COO of Facebook, have both offered the same advice.

In my career, I have witnessed too many times where women shrink, settle back, fade into the background, and surrender their space. If you start watching, you will see it too.

I remember one specific time where I witnessed this very clearly. There was a large presentation with an important partner. The meeting was to be held in our biggest conference room, but it still was not big enough, so we had to try and fit around the conference table, and some were forced to take seats away from the table.

I watched as the women ended up in the back, either by offering their seat at the front of the table to go sit in the back corner or didn't even take a seat at the table at all. They gathered all their materials off the table and sat in the back row, and by doing so, they shrank and faded into the background.

It's so easy to do. In the name of being accommodating, we cross our legs and think, *I don't mind sitting in the back or off in the corner. It won't bother me. I can just hold my papers and laptop on my lap.*

But when you do that, you have lessened your chance of being heard. Stay in the front row. Don't surrender your space. These are the moments when you should pull your chair right up to the table and settle in. You put your elbows on the table and you open your laptop. You are there for a reason.

I understand that if you're a processor, you're probably comfortable with the back row and the corner. This gives you the space to reflect and ponder things. You can still take the space you need to reflect and ponder your contributions while you are at the table. Don't put yourself at a disadvantage before the meetings even start.

The idea of pulling up your chair is a leadership principle to help women work on the skill of confidence. When you dwindle in the corners, you give a visual sign that people's confidence in you should decrease. Others see you as less engaged or relevant, and that is wrong. Your perspective is just as valuable as that of anyone else in the room.

It's harder to join the conversation when you're in the back or the corner. And as a leader, it can be frustrating to see this happen.

I had a regular meeting with several managers who all knew their stuff, and together we tackled significant business issues. I watched while an awesome woman manager stepped back and took a seat at the edge of the room because the meeting was always crowded. She sat and listened quietly rather than being involved.

Then after the meeting, she came into my office with a great question. I wondered, "Why didn't you pose this question during our meeting? It's a great perspective. I would have loved to hear how the team would have debated the question."

I truly valued her participation, especially her insightful questions, but the choices she made to fade into the background deprived us all.

If you have been asked to attend a meeting and you don't contribute, why are you there? When you shrink away, you are placing a burden on your leaders to then have to specifically call you out and ask for your input. And then it gets awkward. Don't get caught off guard. Fading into the background doesn't protect you from that. In fact, it makes it harder for everyone to see you as a part of the team.

Why do we have resistance to something so simple? There is a balance we struggle with. The balance of contributing and speaking up and the negative perceptions of being bold. Sometimes boldness gets interpreted as harsh, rigid, or worse. That's not your problem. If someone tells you that you are being too bossy or too controlling, that is something you can address later with them. It's on them if they take offense when no offense was intended. Bold women have always made weaker people afraid, but that's no excuse. Be bold anyway.

There is a balance we walk between being liked and not liked. Lois Frankel is one of my favorite coaches and authors, and she has been highly influential to me. She said in her book *Nice Girls Don't Get the Corner Office*:

> *Likeability is a critical factor in your success. People get promoted, demoted, hired, and fired based on how likable they are. There's a little girl in all of us who wants to be liked—and there's nothing wrong with that. It's when the needs of the little girl overshadow the rational, adult woman that we get into trouble ... It's critical to understand the difference between being liked and being respected.*

It goes both ways though. Some women think things like "This isn't a popularity contest" and "I'm not here to make friends." But, in reality, you are. You are there to build relationships, to work with a team, and to hit the business objectives you need to work together to make that happen. Frankel elaborated on this:

> *If you're only concerned with being respected and not liked, you lose the support of people you may need in your camp. Paradoxically, it's the people who are liked and respected who are most successful in the workplace.*

Sure, sometimes it's appropriate to be polite and move. It can be the most civil and appropriate thing to do in certain circumstances. But I hope you are not the first one to give up your chair. It's not about being rude. It is about confidence and keeping yourself in the physical space you are in.

There are ways to take up your space in polite but clear ways. I had a client who had an experience with this principle when she was having a conversation with her boss. From the outside, their meeting looked informal because she was standing in the doorway of his office with the door open. But, regardless of the appearance, they were having a meaningful and important conversation and she needed to get his input to solve a problem.

Another team member came up to them and completely barged in, interrupting their meeting. Casually walking in front of her, this coworker carelessly derailed their conversation.

In those moments when we are physically interrupted, we have a tendency to step aside and give them room. I was so proud of her when she did not step aside or walk away. She didn't even move out of the doorway to give them space. She patiently waited for the coworker to finish talking and politely said, "I need to finish the conversation I was having here."

It wasn't rude. It was just a fact. She was confident in her space, and for that, I have no doubt, her boss recognized the leader in her.

Follow her example. Hold your ground. If you need to let someone interrupt you, fine, but then make sure you come back and say, "I wasn't finished."

When we lose that physical space, whether it be when you're standing having a conversation or sitting in a meeting, it makes it harder to exude that confidence that we're already struggling with.

Don't be afraid
Be bold and hold
your ground

Don't be afraid. Be bold, and hold your ground.

Separate the Emotion

Our confidence gets shaken when a person pulls the "I have more experience than you" card. This has happened to me more than once, but one particular instance when I was a president stands out in my memory. My CFO at the time was older than me, but we worked well together. I truly respected his perspective and enjoyed our conversations.

On this day, we were in my office having a conversation about some financial matters. He was not clear on numbers, and neither was I. He gave his reasons for his version of what he thought they should be. I challenged him by asking questions around why I thought the numbers should be higher or lower, all with the intent to have a good dialogue about it.

For some reason, he took it as me asking leading questions because I already knew the answer. I didn't know the answer, but I wanted to. I wanted to work ideas back and forth and come to a solution. And that's when he got frustrated.

He said, "Vicki, I've been doing this since you were in grade school. Why don't you just tell me what you want the number to be?"

It was true. He was a CFO when I was in grade school. But this comment left me speechless. It was condescending and disrespectful. I was mad.

I'm not sure if I handled it correctly, but I responded, "I don't know the number. I think we have to work together on a number, but what you just said was not appropriate. I think we're done for now. We'll come back to this later."

Literally, I was so mad, and, at that time, it was best just to end the conversation. I reflected on this years later and am glad for the lesson that when you're young and moving through your career, if you are being promoted over people with more experience, there are reasons for that. Don't let age or experience downplay your confidence. If anything, it should strengthen it. You're where you are for a reason.

It took me a while to reflect on this after, but there comes a time when your specific experience is greater than those who have more years in experience. I did not want age, gender, or job title to be a reason for me to lose confidence in that moment.

When that CFO treated me like I was a little girl who didn't know anything, there were a number of responses available to me. When emotional moments come up for you, and they will, you also have choices.

First solve the business issue and then separately clarify the emotion.

There are so many times when business issues and emotions come together. Sometimes when we're working through problems, we do get mad or sad. That's natural. Sometimes things happen that are confusing or disrespectful.

During these moments, work to separate the emotion from the conversation and continue to work the business issue.

When you're solving business issues while you are exuding anger or hurt, others may lose confidence in your ability. It's next to impossible to solve the business issue when you are overcome with emotion. You are just seen as too emotional and that you may not understand the business issue at all.

I had a coworker who set the perfect example of this for me once. Stacy overheard her leader talking to someone who worked under her. She heard him talking about another way to solve a problem that she had been working on. His comments gave her the impression that he didn't trust the decisions she was making, and it hurt her to see that he was going around her to express those concerns to someone who worked under her.

Stacy experienced a blend of emotions in that moment from mad to hurt to self-doubt. She wondered if he thought she was working on the wrong things or going about solving problems the wrong way and was taken off guard. She couldn't help wondering, *And why is he talking to her about it? Why isn't he talking to me?*

She was wise enough not to address the emotional issue of going around her and to focus; her first concern was the business issue. She needed to find out if her leader wanted her to realign another way to solve this problem, but she knew she couldn't step into the conversation without the emotion right then.

Fortunately, she had the liberty not to address it right at that moment, so she took a moment to collect herself and to tackle one issue at a time. These are issues that should be addressed relatively quickly, within a day or two. It does no one any good to carry the uncertainty and emotion with you. If you need to address the first issue one day and the second on the next day, that's OK. But don't let it go too long because you will talk yourself out of having the conversation.

A short time later, and in a very calm conversation with her leader, she addressed the business issue and their approach to solving it. She told him she needed to confirm that she and her team were on the right page and that they were moving things forward. And they were. He was totally aligned with what she was doing, but she needed that validation because of what she had heard.

Then she could bring up the emotional issue. Stacy did not have these conversations at the same time. She took a little more time to unpack the issue to lower levels before doing this part so that she did not risk getting overwhelmed and anxious. She went back to him and told him what had happened and how she felt.

She came back to him and said, "I need to talk to you about another issue. I overheard you talking at the watercooler, and I just don't know why you went around me. It felt like you were second-guessing our approach."

She exuded her confidence as she explained her reaction to what she perceived. He was completely taken off guard. He didn't realize that she perceived his actions this way. He just thought he was talking to another coworker at the watercooler. He was just brainstorming ideas but not doubting the direction. It was a complete misalignment of her perception and his intent. Having that conversation brought that back together.

And moving forward, he understood and had more clarity on his conversations with people; he was having an impact beyond what he saw. He didn't take into account he was a vice president stepping over his manager.

They had a really good conversation and came back into alignment. Their relationship was better moving forward, so it was a win-win for all.

Easier said than done, though. It's hard because, dang it, we're emotional! I mean, we've all cried at work. We know we're not supposed to, but we do. It happens. What's important is that if you are emotional at work—let's say if you do actually cry or raise your voice—you should come back and explain the emotion. Come back and put words to why you were emotional instead of just letting people guess. You don't want people to assume what may have caused your emotion. They will never get it right.

You can do it right in the moment if it makes sense for you and your culture. You could say, "OK, I really believe in this initiative and that's why I'm getting emotional" or "This meeting is running long, and I have to get my kid from daycare at six o'clock, so I'm getting anxious about this." I mean, there are reasons for your emotion. If you can explain it in the moment, great. If not, come back and explain it.

By being able to pull the issues apart and deal with them one at a time, we create a greater sense of confidence. You can do it.

Do It Anyway

The principle of "do it anyway" is the bedrock of my career. Don't give in to that voice in your head that says, "You're not ready. You can't do this."

It happens to everyone. Know those feelings of doubt are there when they come. Recognize them but then have the courage to continue to move forward with that head held high, shoulders back, and with a firm tone of competence in your voice. I lost track of how many times I didn't feel I was ready to do something hard or intimidating, but I had to do it anyway.

In hindsight, when I "did it anyway," were those moments perfect? No, but those were the moments that strengthened and developed my confidence. As some say, if you're going to fail, fail fast, continuing to learn and grow.

Those are the moments that you can exude your value; even though you may not feel 100 percent ready, do it anyway. But as you do, be true to yourself. Don't try to be something different than what you are. It's just being able to share what you've got. And what you've got is awesome.

When you do it anyway, you exude confidence, and you build confidence. Feeling an emotion and exuding it are two different things. You can feel anxious but still work hard not to exude anxiousness. That is about holding your center, and this is where the executive presence comes in, which we'll talk about in chapter six. Hang in there with me!

Too often, women seem to believe that other people have more influence over us than we have on ourselves. We think, *I'm going to wait to speak until I'm spoken to.* I encourage you to stop doing that. Force yourself to think, *If two minutes of time is available to me, I will take my two minutes.*

There are times that we're caught off guard and we don't know how to respond. No matter how long I've been doing this, I am still faced with self-doubt. I should have known better, but sometimes my nerves got the best of me. Those are the moments that linger with me still. They are the growing moments.

Not too long ago, I found myself in a very formal environment with around forty leaders that I really didn't know that well. There was a casual ten minutes before a very important meeting was to begin, and I was one of probably three females.

I tried to mingle and get to know these people, but I couldn't find a way to fit into the conversations. They all knew each other and were discussing topics that made it feel like I couldn't just slide myself into the conversation. I felt like I stuck out like a sore thumb, standing there and feeling so incompetent. I totally lost my confidence.

At this point in my career, my panic took me by surprise.

I went to the bathroom because I knew there'd be no one there. I set my bag on the sink, took a moment to fix my lipstick, and looked in the mirror. I literally said to myself, "Vicki, you're going to do this again. Let's go."

And I did. I walked back in the room, held my head up, and smiled at everyone I saw. I walked up to a group and said, "Which division do you work for?"

The panic faded away because I forced myself to get a grip. I did it anyway. Sure, I had to give myself that moment to find my big girl pants. But I got back out there. We all have those moments where we need to talk back to the voice in our head.

Be Your Authentic Self

The final principle for confidence is to be your authentic self. The stupid labels some women put on themselves are so limiting that it makes me furious. They use terms like: imposter syndrome, bossy, bitchy, shy, weak, know-it-all, etc. Don't let any of those words be a part of your vocabulary. You only have to be you, and that's all.

In our society, girls are still told to go play nice. We are given signals that it's better to be seen and not heard or whatever. Don't be too loud. Don't make a scene. Fit in. All that stuff. That may have not been your specific upbringing, but these tendencies still exist in our culture. I have seen evidence of that attitude lingering with so many women as they go through their professional careers.

The pressures of work, particularly as you become a leader, will present you with challenges where you feel like you have to be someone or something else. My advice is that when this happens, go back to your value statement. Reflect on what you're good at, what you enjoy doing, who you are. Hold your head high. Don't let the pressure to change get to you.

I was sitting at a board dinner one night, which was wonderful. It gave me an opportunity to get to know these board members in a more social environment at a nice, big round table. The conversation around the table was about vacations and social events and things of that nature. I wasn't participating a whole lot in the conversation because I was exhausted. I had just flown in from Wisconsin and had to hurry and get to this dinner.

Here I was, sitting in this elegant place, listening to the board members discuss whatever it was they were discussing. And all I could think was, *Did someone shovel the driveway?* Back home, it had snowed, and it was a concern of mine at the moment.

> *When we act like someone we're not that erodes our confidence*

Now someone would say that that is imposter syndrome. But screw that. It is not imposter syndrome. I belonged at that table, so I deserved to be there. Just because my frame of thinking was different than theirs didn't make me any less. My concern about shoveling the driveway was a part of my real and authentic life.

When we act like someone we're not, that erodes our confidence. It's that simple. Be you.

Having It ALL:
Actionable Leadership Lessons

Confidence is a skill, and like all other skills, you need practice before it's perfected. As you work through the less confident moments, you build your confidence skill. It can start as simply as stepping a little outside your comfort zone. Each time you take a little risk and push yourself, you will find that you will become more comfortable taking your space and contributing. You will find the joy of being you and enjoy the confidence you have with the value you bring.

When challenges arise—and they will—don't let them get to you. Focus on one issue at a time, and separate the business issues from those that are causing emotions. But tackle and solve each systematically.

Do it anyway!

Suggested Actions:

- Take your space and hold your ground. And be the kind of leader who includes everyone. When you are presented with the temptation to shrink to the sidelines, stay put and ask the group, "How will we keep everyone here involved?"

- Start a thought journal. A thought journal is a way of recording your thoughts and reflecting on the specific business issues vs. the emotion of those issues. It's designed to help you reflect on the emotion by finding a more balanced way of thinking about things. Include these components:

- What was the situation?

- What was the emotion? Why?

- What were your immediate thoughts?

- Can I define the facts?

- Reflect on what you know now. What could have been more effective?

Download the free journaling worksheets or purchase the reflection guide workbook at **www.vickiupdike.com/ navigatingyourjourney**.

CHAPTER FOUR

Be Heard

It Isn't About Talking Louder

I come from a family of talkers.

At meals, we don't ever leave any silence on the table. We all talk over each other, and if you want to be heard, you just talk louder. Whenever I brought people home who didn't know us very well, they would get kind of stressed out. Friends of mine have had to take breaks because there was so much talking. Our spouses are lucky if they get a word in. It's chaos. It's fun. And that's what we're comfortable with. That's just the way we are.

As it always happens, I didn't realize we were this way until I left home and came back. Sitting at dinner, I noticed for the first time that there were always three or four people talking at the same time.

At work, I started to notice that I communicated the same way. When I felt like I wasn't being heard, I just notched things up. I talked louder. I took over the conversation and changed the subject when I wanted to talk about something different. That was my learned behavior.

As a result of my communication style, people started tuning me out. Until I stopped and took a good look at myself, I had no idea that I came across as overbearing and impatient. I realized my way was not necessarily effective in the workplace. Adjusting how I communicate has been a hard lesson but a valuable one. It took some time to unlearn those old habits, but I did.

Now when I go back home and sit at those same family dinners, I sit back and smile.

Have you ever had that experience where you have a great idea and share it, and it seems to fall on deaf ears? And then five minutes later, someone else says something kind of similar and everybody starts rallying around that idea. And you're left thinking, *Hello? Am I sitting in this chair? Am I at this meeting? Did anyone hear the words I just said?*

The answer is yes, they're hearing the words you say, but are they truly listening to you? I want to give you specific, actionable steps you can take that will give you a better chance of being heard and having your influence felt by those around you.

Being heard is not just about talking. It includes subtle choices in how we talk and how we communicate. It's about creating influence through the way we choose our words, the way we deliver those words, and through the times we choose not to speak. These may sound like small things, but they can be very significant to the impact, particularly as you share ideas and make contributions.

Be Prepared

Preparedness brings strength and confidence that what you have to say is important and valuable. This ties back to knowing your value. To show your confidence, I always encourage women to be one of the first to speak in meetings. Don't wait. When you're prepared and ready to go, there's no reason to sit on the sidelines and wait for someone else to get things started. Just put yourself out there.

Easily said, I know. It takes practice. It can be frustrating, especially if you're not used to doing this. There are times you're going to walk away from a failed interaction and think, *That was horrible.* But with practice, there will be more and more times you're going to walk away from conversations with your head held up and think, *I was awesome!*

We live in a busy world. We work in a busier world. We are going from meeting to meeting or Zoom to Zoom, and it is hectic. That is not an excuse to show up unprepared.

Being prepared means more than just being technically competent. It means being able to articulate your thoughts and ideas in those moments that you're given. This means reading the reports that are sent ahead, knowing the emails and conversations that have happened, looking at the agenda, and showing up to the premeeting before the meeting. If there's someone you need to talk to so you can come to the meeting being prepared, do that.

If you are not prepared, then you will be less engaged in the meeting and will not contribute as much as you could. This has an effect on the way you are perceived by those you work with.

Don't get me wrong. We're not always in every meeting to solve the world's problems. I know that not participating in a meeting may work sometimes, and may even be necessary. But choose carefully those meetings where you are less engaged. Don't make a habit of standing on the sidelines because when the time comes when you want to be heard and the stakes are higher, nobody will hear you.

That moment when you really need to contribute is not the time for you to lose your confidence. It is in those moments that you need to know you are worthy of the conversation. There is a reason you're on the team. When you are prepared, you can seize the opportunity to contribute when you need it.

If you don't have an addition in these conversations, ask a question. If you don't have content to share, it's OK for you to be inquisitive. It doesn't look unprepared to say, "Tell me more. That idea sounds really interesting." This way it's not just about you and your ideas. You're also bringing the ideas out of others.

Preparedness looks different for every person. I know people who can read a financial report ten minutes before walking into a meeting and they're prepared. That's awesome for them. That's the way they do it. I always needed a little more time. I knew if I needed to understand something complex before a meeting, I needed to see it a couple hours ahead of time. That was what prepared looked like for me. I requested what I needed in the timeline that made sense for me to have it. I spent time quietly reviewing and pondering on that information so that I clearly understood what the important issues were and what my contribution would be regarding them.

Preparedness allows you to be confident, and that confidence leads to being heard

Knowing what I thought and what I wanted to say before every meeting brought me calmness. And that calmness led to security and confidence that I could exude. It is the same for you. Preparedness allows you to be confident, and that confidence leads to being heard.

Believe in yourself because you're worthy to be listened to. In previous chapters, I talked about the importance of believing in yourself and knowing your value. This is the next step. We all have internal barriers where we don't think anyone wants to hear our ideas. Your preparedness brings self-assurance.

Creating Airtime

The phrase "creating airtime" means finding a way to be heard in a cluttered conversation. This idea was a foreign concept to me. In my family, you don't create airtime. When you want to say something, you just talk over anyone else who happens to be talking.

There are times when you want to add something into a group conversation or a meeting but there's a cadence going that doesn't seem to allow you that chance. Even though you want to jump in, you just can't find a pocket. It's not that people are necessarily being rude. They might simply be excited and there's an energy happening that is carrying things along at a fast clip. How do you make a space for yourself when this happens?

First, ask yourself why you can't break in. Maybe you're just not an aggressive personality or maybe you were taught it was rude. There was a man on my team once who was really uncomfortable interrupting or jumping in too fast. This was just against his nature, so he struggled with the kinds of meeting like I just described.

As teammates, we all knew this about him. The solution was that he actually came up with a little hand gesture where he'd simply raise his hand up and away from his wrist, sort of like a little ramp. It was a signal that he wanted to on-ramp into the conversation. We all knew that when we saw his fingers pop up, we needed to make space for him to speak. It was an elegant solution.

You may find a similar strategy useful as well if you find this happening on your team. It doesn't have to be a hand signal. It might be a clearing of the throat or a phrase that you interject: "I don't want to interrupt you, but I have something to say …" In some circumstances, a shifted body posture such as leaning forward and putting your hands on the table may be all it takes. These kinds of simple signals can be really helpful in your team environment, and regardless of your title, you can embrace them and lead others in recognizing how effective they can be.

There are times when subtlety won't do, environments where you don't necessarily have that option. When this happens, you have to watch the natural cadence and flow of the conversation. Being prepared helps you in this space because there's not going to be a lot of downtime between inputs in these conversations. You have to be ready to grab the next beat when it happens and just jump in.

This may be uncomfortable to you, but I want you to try it anyway. You can find a way to be heard. Best solution is still to be one of the first to speak up. Even if it's just in your Zoom meetings. I have noticed we're less interrupted in our virtual world than in our actual world. But it still happens.

Take Back the Credit

I remember a specific meeting when I was pretty young in my career. I knew everybody around the table, and I knew that the topic we were talking about was really important. I knew there would be presidents and vice presidents in attendance, so I came prepared for the discussion. I wanted to make a contribution and show that I was technically competent.

When it was my turn to speak, I was ready to go and confidently began to share what I was prepared to share. Ten words in, I was interrupted. I immediately fell back onto myself and gave up. I didn't contribute for the rest of the meeting.

At the time, I didn't have the gumption to step back in and say something. The person who interrupted me didn't know they had done that to me, and I certainly didn't correct them. But I look back now and know that I can do better. I was there to contribute. I was there to bring my perspective. And although I tried, that was a lost opportunity for me to exude my talents to this group of important people.

This happens all the time. Start watching and you're bound to see it. Getting interrupted can completely deflate your ability to continue to contribute. But when this happens, I want you to be ready. I don't want you to regret not contributing.

Let's take this common scenario first. It seems like there is always the one person who interrupts others on a consistent basis, and for some mysterious reason, people let them. A client of mine noticed one particular individual consistently swayed the conversation in every meeting by interrupting everyone and then rambling on in an unrelated way. She kicked herself for letting her contributions get swallowed up in this person's conversation. She knew it needed to end, but she didn't know what to do about it. These meetings were important, and she almost always came with questions she needed answers to that were never addressed. She would go back to her desk and feel defeated. It was a waste of everyone's time.

She prepared herself well and decided it was time to try something new. At the next meeting, the interrupter predictably took the floor. But she stayed in her space, let the person interrupt, and then, rather than resign herself to defeat as she and everyone else had always done, she politely and boldly said, "I need to finish my point."

She was a mild personality, so this took everything she had. For one thing, she got the answers she needed, and for another, the meeting stayed on track and ended on time. And most importantly, it gave her a new measure of confidence. She walked out of that meeting feeling really awesome about herself. She knew she didn't have to wait anymore to have the conversations she needed to have.

Every business has its own culture, and that influences our communication style. That's OK, but don't let it stop you from being heard. It doesn't mean that you don't have the opportunity to jump in with casual confidence after the interrupter takes a breath and say, "I want to finish my point."

Let's examine another common situation. You've probably had times when you say something and then someone interrupts you and starts saying the same exact thing. Or maybe fifteen minutes later, someone repeats your thought again. What do you do?

I want you to take back the credit. Don't let them steal your thunder. You can kindly say, "Thank you for bringing that up again" or "I mentioned that a bit ago, and I really like that idea." Or you could say, "Thank you for supporting my idea and bringing it back to the table."

Be gracious about this. It is a good idea to acknowledge that the person made a contribution, but help them recognize that it was the second time that that contribution was added. It isn't about being mean or being stubborn or being a know-it-all. It's about those little subtle things that send meaningful signals that allow you to get the credit you deserve.

I've been on the receiving side of this, and I am a little embarrassed to admit I have also been on the giving end. There have been times when I was "already listening." I thought I already knew what they were going to say. We'll talk more about listening in the next chapter, but I want to share one story when I realized how easy it is to unconsciously fall into this habit and how one marvelous woman handled me graciously when I took the credit that belonged to her.

I was in a meeting, and, as sometimes happens, the conversation evolved into a brainstorming session. As the leader of the group at this time, I joined in and contributed some of my ideas. After a few minutes, I presented a "really great" idea. Everyone seemed to grab a hold of it, and the discussion turned in that direction.

People listen to you a little bit more when you are in a leadership role. I don't like that this is the case, but it is. Nobody pointed out there was a problem with my great idea. The problem was it wasn't mine.

Without realizing it, I had reiterated an idea made by another woman earlier. At which point, she said, "Thank you, Vicki, for saying that again. You know, I really believe in that idea."

And I literally took a little gasp and thought, *Oh my gosh! I am not listening. How disrespectful of me.*

I knew I should have known better. I should have been listening and acknowledged the contributions that she made at the time she made them. I totally took it away from her. Like I said, old habits die hard.

But she spoke up, I recognized my mistake, and she properly took back the credit for her idea. And that was where we left it. We all knew she did the right thing. I was thankful she was confident enough to speak up because it sent the right signal to me and everyone there.

These aren't monumental moments that you're having throughout your career; they're just these little subtle flashes. But, over time, those seemingly small conversations and choices can have a much larger impact—on you, on your teams, and on your entire organization.

Use of Humor

Humor has a lot of benefits. It can make your workplace an enjoyable place to be. It reduces stress. It gets people to listen. It fosters a rapport. It creates connections. Using humor builds trust and even can diffuse conflict. There are a lot of good things that come with humor as long as it is used appropriately.

Don't use humor to hide an issue or to downplay an idea. Putting humor around something that matters may make you look like you don't have an understanding of the true impact of the issue. It can minimize the significant issues.

What you may feel is funny may actually be hurtful to someone else. I was on a team that got along really well. We all had those little nuances that we all knew of each other, and we'd pick those out in meetings. It was humorous, but I didn't realize that, over time, one of our team members actually felt like they were a bit of the butt of our jokes. Of course, that was not the intent of our jokes, but it had a negative impact anyway. They started shutting down and were less likely to share their ideas.

When we realized what was happening, our team added a new policy in our team operating procedures. We added a line about using humor appropriately because we didn't want to embarrass anyone with humor. We didn't want to hide our issues in humor. We wanted to make sure that in those moments, we were communicating clearly without inappropriate humor and sarcasm.

When we're trying to take back the credit or make a point, some women choose a sarcastic comment or misplaced humor. Never use sarcasm to make light of something. Sarcasm rarely works. Particularly when it's yourself that you are talking about. That is a way of infusing doubt and doesn't add to your professionalism.

I will be the first to tell you my faults, but that's not necessarily a good characteristic in all situations. Making fun of myself is fine in the right settings, but in the wrong ones, it means minimizing my contributions. The use of self-deprecating humor can be very counterproductive.

We've all done this, I'd bet. In one important presentation, I stood up, and the first thing I did was apologize for my lack of skills in PowerPoint. I told everyone my presentation was "simple." I made a needless apology (which I'm going to talk about later in this chapter), and I also made fun of my technical skills.

This is an example of the inappropriate use of humor. It was completely the wrong message to start with for the content that I was presenting. I was trying to joke, but it wasn't even a joke. It was ridiculous. I apologized for something that I shouldn't have. The contents of the slides were just fine. Sure, I wish they looked more polished, but I just don't have those skills. It may have been funny to some, but I risked losing my credibility with the group for a cheap laugh. That was not my best self.

Humor can be risky when the clarity of a point is at stake. There are times when you need to make a clear point, and the tone and the cadence of those conversations are different. When you do need to make an important point, don't crowd it with humor. Let your message stand for itself.

Slow Your Words

Sometimes women feel that it's rude to take up too much time, so we talk fast to get everything in. We are self-conscious about the amount of time we take, so we tend to quickly throw our words out there.

Another problem we have is when we're only allotted a certain amount of time. Sometimes when this happens, we rush to fill the time slot we have been given. Because of this, we lose the point in the rambling of our words.

Instead of clarifying what we want to say, we just talk faster. This is the opposite of an effective delivery. Speeding up actually diminishes your point. When you slow down, your point is made with clarity. People know what they are supposed to hear.

I've been in team meetings where we go around the table and give updates. (Side note: I don't recommend this for agenda items since it's the biggest waste of time!) Early in my career, I always thought that what I had to say was pretty darn important, so I made sure I used my full allotment of time. I talked fast and I read a lot of numbers off my papers. I wanted to show how much I was getting done.

The first time I presented a marketing strategy, I was given forty-five minutes. Here I was, this eager executive who wanted to show that she deserved a spot at the table. I was ready. I had my slides all set to go. I had practiced my presentation.

Then I got up there and went through it so quickly it was all a blur. I finished in thirty minutes.

In both of these examples, nobody heard a word I said. I barely paused to breathe because I didn't want anybody to interrupt me. It was like I was back at my old kitchen table back at home.

How silly did I look? In both these cases, that was definitely a less effective approach. I didn't appreciate who I was talking to, and I wasn't clear about the point I wanted them to hear.

I didn't realize how hard it can be to listen to fast talkers. Everyone probably walked out of those meetings exhausted. Worse, they probably saw a nervous executive up there who struggled to get to the point. This habit took a long time to break.

To avoid the wrong impression, make sure that the issues and the topics you share are given the right pace. Don't try to dazzle them with speed. Find a good cadence by pacing your words. I have learned over time, and even my kids know this today, when I slow my words and start talking softer, that is a signal that what I am saying is more important. It's the impact of timing and volume.

Speaking slowly and calmly gives a signal that you are not overly reactionary or overly impulsive. Thoughtfulness is exuded in the way you sound. So if you think you might be a fast talker and there is a risk of people tuning you out, my advice is to take a breath and bring it down a level.

Get to the Point

I once worked with a fabulous VP of finance who was so technically solid. Everyone depended on him. But when you asked him a question, he never gave a straight answer. He gave this whole preamble to what he was thinking about, somewhere in there he would answer your question, and then he pontificated afterward. You got the entire thought process on why he was coming up with the answer he was in the moment. It was always a whole long story about why he might be right or he might be wrong, and why there were other options to think about. Half the time, I didn't even know where to find the answer in all those words.

Listening to someone like that is exhausting. The endless on-ramps and off-ramps, the pre- and post-ideas, wear us out, and the message usually gets lost. Rambling and overexplaining dilutes your point. In the workplace, if someone asks you a direct question, start your conversation with a direct answer. If it's a yes or no question, start with a yes or no answer. If it's a true or false question, answer true or false. Don't verbally wander.

Too often, people talk to fill gaps. When nobody says anything, we needlessly fill the air with words that don't mean anything. We all know when this happens, we tune out. Rambling loses people.

Don't be afraid of silence. If you find that you are repeating yourself just to take up airtime, stop. Sometimes we are given five minutes, and we feel we have to continue to say something for all of those minutes, even if we only have three minutes' worth of information to share. So we drone on, and it gets to a point where we never end. We lose track of exactly what we're saying and then we kind of just let it drift off and wait for someone to interrupt.

This is so ridiculous. It's actually bolder to simply end. Provide silence for a minute and give yourself that moment. It is a hard habit to break, but it can be such a relief to those who are listening to you.

For so many people, especially those who naturally are rambling idea-drivers, silence does make us uncomfortable. We feel we should continue to fill the space, but keep in mind, there are times when the point needs to end. If nobody is ready to pick up the conversation when it ends, that's OK. Often that means people are listening and need time to consider your point. That is an impactful use of time. Allow the silent space.

With that said, I know a lot of women tend to be verbal processors. Have you ever heard the saying "I don't know what I think until I see what I say"? This kind of thinking-out-loud process can be really useful, particularly when you are debating ideas or trying to understand scope. These are diverging conversations where it's OK for you to ramble a bit and just say words to say words.

Consider how collaborative brainstorming sessions can turn into great moments to really come together and gel. There is a real excitement in those environments. These are situations where talking over each other is actually a good thing. It can create energy and ideas. It's

OK to suggest you all play ball with an idea and leave room for that in these conversations, but it's good to make it clear that that's what the conversation is. Even in more formal environments, it's OK to say, "Can we talk this through a little more?" and let your mind and words wander a bit.

But when people come to you for something, give them the something. You don't need to pontificate or philosophize about it. In these instances, you don't want to appear to be the rambling idea-driver. Have discernment as to which situations are appropriate for lengthy discussions and which are not. You can be comfortable bringing every conversation to a thoughtful place.

Being clear and getting to the point is the most important way to be heard

Being clear and direct is the most important component of being heard. This reduces the cloudiness around our conversations. Believe in yourself; start with your main message. Know your point and communicate it plainly. You can give reasons and information to support that message after, but give it first and end with it. This may be the biggest lesson I have to offer in this whole book, so I'll repeat it. Being clear and getting to the point is the most important way to be heard.

Don't Diminish Your Message

CLARIFYING WORDS

I want to talk a little bit about clarifying words. All of these disclaimers or these preambles we tend to use before giving our ideas or our thoughts are doing us a disservice. We have to stop diminishing the confidence others have in us by using language to our disadvantage.

First, don't start your comments with a negative: "This might be a stupid question but …" or "I'm just going to throw something out there, and it's probably way off …" or "I could be wrong, but …" or "Does anyone like this idea?" or, my least favorite, "Can you do me a favor?"

Those kinds of statements cast doubt when there's no reason to cast doubt. Do you really need a favor? Do you really think you're wrong? No! Be bold and own your words without disparaging them before they are even spoken.

If you're telling people it's going to be stupid, they're already starting to think it's stupid before you say anything else. One of my pet peeves is the word "just." It is the most overused clarifying word. You hear it everywhere:

"I think we should just …" or "I was just thinking …" or "I have just one idea …" or "Should we just do …" This is such an unnecessary clarifying word because it minimizes everything we're going to say. Compare the examples I just shared with these: "I think we should …" and "I was thinking …" and "I have an idea …" and "Should we do …"

Do you feel the shift in tone? It is direct and conveys far more confidence. I would really appreciate it if you'd take the word "just" out of your vocabulary.

There are alternative phrases you can use that will convey more confidence and presence. "I suggest" is a great start. So are phrases like "My plan is …" and "I recommend …" and "My preference is …" But I want to add a warning. So many women change their tone when using these sorts of phrases. They almost sing it: "Hey, how about X, Y, Z?" We let our voices go up and speak in a higher octave by the end. Is it that girly nature in us? I don't know. But keep the tone of your voice at your normal level and you'll be surprised how different you feel.

You may have actually been taught to use these words so that you don't offend people by bossing them around or telling them what to do. It comes from the therapy world.

Remember your value, your perspective is important.

I recommend replacing "I feel" with "I believe" or "I know." You can tell people that this is your perspective. Make those points stronger. Clarifying words diminish your point. So it's almost like saying, "I'm not sure this is good. I probably shouldn't even say this." And by so doing, you diminish the confidence others have in the idea that you're presenting.

And please, whatever you do, don't phrase your thoughts as questions. This phenomenon has grown in popularity so much that it has an official title—uptalk. Women and girls tend to do it more than men and boys. They phrase their sentences as though there was a question mark at the end of every one instead of a period. "I'd like to report on the results of this quarter?" "Excuse me, I need to take this call?" Give your words the respect they deserve by communicating them appropriately.

EXPRESSION

Our nonverbal communication is as important as our verbal communication. Shelves of books have been written on this topic. I want to call out one specific form of nonverbal expression I notice women doing a lot, and that is smiling inappropriately.

Being expressive is OK. We're women. We like to smile. That is fine. But we don't always think about how our facial expressions need to align with the message we are delivering.

Let me explain what I mean. I feel a little foolish remembering this, but it illustrates the point well. As a new executive, we didn't do well one quarter and I had to present these disappointing results to the board of directors. It was my first time sharing a bit of a business failure, so I did what I always did and just got up there and cheerfully delivered the message. I'm up there, smiling away, sharing the not-so-good news. If I had a video of that moment, I'm sure I would be shocked at how mismatched my facial expression was to the heavy message I was delivering.

Women do this all the time. Body language can discredit your words very quickly. People have to wonder, "Do you truly understand the impact of what you're saying? Do you know the scope of the problem?"

We come by it honestly, I know. It's no wonder we smile. When men don't smile, they're taken seriously. When women don't smile, we're asked what's wrong. No wonder we smile. I am not saying we have to change our culture, but I do want you to consider how important it is for your facial expressions to match the message. Watch how much you smile when you are sharing weighty information. I want to encourage you to match your facial expression with the content of your speech.

OVER-APOLOGIZING

Women tend to apologize when we don't need to. OK, not just sometimes. All the time. It's so common that people have written whole books about it as well. Don't apologize for your presence and your perspectives. Don't diminish your contributions.

I'm here to tell you that apologizing for unintentional things diminishes your perceived competence. Have awareness of those moments when you're not sure what to do but you are trying to figure it out.

We do this in very weird ways as women. We do it so much, like a nervous habit. I don't even think we hear ourselves: "I'm sorry, but I have one more point." You know, that kind of thing. Like we're taking up too much time and have to apologize for our very presence. Don't worry about it! If you have something to say, just say it.

Sometimes we use apologizing to soften the message, but there's ways to soften the message without apologizing. Rather than saying "I'm sorry, but I don't agree with you," you don't have to just say, "I don't agree." That can be too harsh. You can say, "I have a different perspective that I'd like to share." It's OK for you to have an opinion. Rather than saying "I apologize for taking up so much time," you can say, "I have a little more to add, and then I'd like to hear what everyone else has to share."

I have a problem with apologizing. I mean, all I have to do is search for the word "sorry" in my sent box and it comes up in nearly every other email. So I know I over-apologize. And I've been working on this for a long time. It's a really tough habit to break because it infiltrates every moment of our lives. Recently, I was walking on a path near where I live, and I was coming up to a blind corner. This little boy on a bike came around too fast and we almost collided because we didn't see each other, but we almost bumped into each other.

I said, "Oh, I'm sorry."

And he waved, said, "It's OK," and rode off.

I walked away laughing at myself, "I did it again. I had nothing to be sorry about. Nobody was hurt. Why did I apologize?"

But it takes away from the times when we truly are sorry. Over-apologizing diminishes the apology. Apologize for things you're truly apologetic for. If you are late getting back to someone, you don't always need to apologize for that. Do men always apologize for being busy? You can simply say, "Thank you for your patience. I appreciate that." And move on.

Don't let bad habits diminish your message and keep you from being heard.

Having It ALL:
Actionable Leadership Lessons

Being clear and direct is the most important factor in being heard, and when you are heard, you have a greater chance of being respected and making a difference.

There's a balance to strike when you're working to be heard. It's your smile. It's your space at the table. It's how you sound and the pace of your words. It is not about talking louder; I tried that. It did not work.

Start and end your message with your point and never downplay your perspective or hide it in humor. Take back the credit and redirect the credit when appropriate. Match your body language to the message.

Suggested Actions:

- Take back control of your calendar. Look through your calendar and create specific blocks of time appropriate for you to prepare and mark them in the calendar. Designate intentional time to clarify your perspective.

- In the next two weeks, find an opportunity for a premeeting. Intentionally seek the perspective of a coworker on an agenda topic prior to the meeting. Share your perspective and ask for feedback.

- The next time your boss comes to you with a question, give them an answer first before you say anything else.

Add additional detail if necessary and then answer the question again.

- Go back to your thought journal and document how you felt. What went right and what went wrong?

- Make a habit of being the first or second to speak up at meetings.

Download the free journaling worksheets or purchase the reflection guide workbook at **www.vickiupdike.com/ navigatingyourjourney**.

CHAPTER FIVE

Thinking Strategically

Too often, women are given the feedback that we need to be more strategic. We're told this when we're passed up for promotions. We are told this in performance reviews. It's something that I've been told myself.

It's not like we are given a lesson on strategic thinking. All this leaves us wondering, *What the heck even is strategic thinking and how do I do it?* What does "more strategic" look like?

I had the chance to reconnect with a past leader of mine. We had a quiet moment to reminisce, so I seized the chance to pick his brain. I had always been impressed with his talent of finding high performers in the organization and leaning on them to do what they did best. He was a master at this. I asked him what it was that they exuded that helped him see this potential.

His answer was simple. "They saw around the corner."

That sentence really resonated with me. He saw the ability in others to see beyond what they do and to understand impact. Strategic thinkers.

When it comes to strategic thinking, there are really two parts: being and doing. By "being," I mean having the mentality of a strategic thinker, and by "doing," I mean demonstrating it. Create the strategic thinker in you AND show people that value. Half of this chapter falls under the "be" category, and the other half is the "do." But before we can go there, we have to define what the term means.

Defining Strategic Thinking

I was coaching an intelligent woman who was technically competent and looking to move her career forward in leadership. But every time she tried to move up, she was told she wasn't strategic enough.

This feedback baffled her because she knew that she could do the job better than anyone in the organization. It threw her back because she was skilled and capable. She couldn't figure out why she was not perceived as strategic. We started working together on defining what strategic thinking actually was.

Strategic thinking is essentially the ability to think theoretically and realistically about a concept, issue, or opportunity. Strategic thinkers can see and understand future impacts of choices while remaining grounded in the present. In other words, it's seeing beyond the task or issue at hand to the longer-term consequences. Strategic thinking is seeing beyond today and our specific tasks by creating a greater perspective.

Strategic thinkers get out of their silo, think beyond the scope, and bring ideas forward in a way that is vulnerable, collaborative, and thoughtful. They look for success.

So many people are focused on the tasks at hand, what needs to be done, and miss the opportunity to understand the impact of the tasks. What are the ultimate outcomes?

Our days are filled with tasks, and it feels good to check them off. There are times we need to rise above the tasks themselves and think about what we are actually trying to accomplish. This is a key aspect of strategic thinking. Pull yourself out of the tasks for a little while. What are you actually trying to achieve? Think from a greater perspective. Am I working on what matters most?

To be a strategic thinker, you need to understand your impact and your influence beyond what you see today. Consider the task beyond your scope.

In one instance, a marketing team I worked with had a task every month to move data in a spreadsheet. It was literally just deleting three columns and forwarding it to someone in IT. There had to be a better way to share information than cutting and pasting columns in a spreadsheet.

Part of effective strategic thinking is to understand the links between tasks, to ask questions like "What does the person in IT do with this information?" and "How is this information needed to continue to run the marketing campaigns so when customers place orders, everything works correctly?" In my instance, we discovered they just needed a small component of the data in the spreadsheet to enter into the system.

As a result, we realized that we, as marketers, could go into the system and put that information there ourselves instead of creating a whole separate file to send. The IT department welcomed this change because it streamlined the process and put the accountability in the right place. Asking and answering the question led to a better solution for all, but it took challenging the "that's the way we've always done it" answer.

I know this sounds so simple, but so often the best things are. Looking back, it's kind of comical, honestly. We were making it so much more complicated than it needed to be. But when you don't understand why you're doing things, you can't find those plain-as-the-nose-on-your-face kinds of solutions.

> When you don't understand why you're doing things, you can't find those plain-as-the-nose-on-your-face kinds of solutions.

Strategic thinking can also include thinking outside what we expect of ourselves and each other as teammates. I once had the wonderful opportunity to take a standardized personality test along with everyone else on my team. Activities like this are great team-building opportunities, which I highly recommend. It was so cool to be able to look at how our personalities impacted the way we thought and how we worked as a group.

This particular test ranked people on a number of indicators, one of which was the "conceptual" vs. "tactical" spectrum. It was no surprise when my results came back showing I was very tactical in my approach to problems.

We had a team-building activity after this where we were divided into two groups: those with high tactical scores (myself included) vs. those with high conceptional scores.

The two teams were each given half of the conference room and told to "build a space station." That was pretty much it. With very little direction, my team grabbed our markers and started drawing plans on the whiteboard. We even had a former pilot on our team, so he figured out where the spacecraft was going to land on our space station. We had living quarters, working quarters, and everything like that all figured out in our plans.

After ten minutes, the facilitator told us to put our pens down. We looked over at the other team, and they were chewing on the ends of their markers, wondering, "So why are we in space?" Their whiteboard was still white. They had been concentrating on figuring out the whole point of going to space before they could move forward making plans for the station.

I never imagined our team had such extremes, but I was so grateful we did because I saw that both ends of the spectrum are needed to be a true strategic thinker. Some of us went off and built the space station. Some of us wondered why we were even going to space. We needed both the thinker and the doer to be a strategic thinker.

That space station exercise made a huge difference moving forward as a team. We reflected back on that conversation for years. Whenever things stalled, we'd say, "Oh, you are still wondering why we're going to space." That was our way of making room for the intuitive thinker. We celebrated the inquisitive nature of finding blind spots.

This was an important lesson for me. I realized that I lean toward moving quickly. That was my natural tendency, so I needed to consciously work to apply the intuitive traits that didn't come as easily to me. Too often in meetings, I thought, *I'm bored with this. I want to keep moving on.* To be a strong strategic thinker, I needed a balance of both, to intentionally slow down and understand things in a broader way.

Elevate your strategic thinking. Probe, listen, and clarify. Ask the questions to help exude your thoughtfulness.

Be Intentional About Your Inquisitive Nature

To find those meaningful connections, one should be creatively inquisitive, seeking to understand issues, problems, and opportunities from a broader perspective.

Strategic thinkers like to get to the root cause and identify impactful solutions. They seek to understand things from other perspectives and consider biases that maybe nobody is questioning. There is a very simple way to do this: ask questions. Get outside your bubble. Investigate. Go out and seek other perspectives. Use that network.

If you encounter a very established process, seek to understand. You don't have to be irritating, just curious. If you have those moments of "why?" that's a good place to dwell. This curiosity builds your ability to be a strategic thinker and see beyond the task at hand. Don't be satisfied with "We've always done it this way." Answer the why.

When being inquisitive, you are trying to collect information—as much as you can—to fully assess whatever it is you're working on. It's not finding the solution yet. Sometimes we get stubborn about defending our own ideas, but being inquisitive means we truly have to consider other perspectives.

This curiosity will help to form many options, and then use all those options to make a decision about the best next step moving forward. Of course, it's not just about the decision; it's about the future. It's about getting the results for success of that issue or opportunity. You can and will create stronger solutions and continue to create that network of people who you want to work with. Who doesn't want to be asked their opinions?

There are times when you have to rise above the tasks and think about the outcome of what you are all really trying to do. What defines success? What drives this success? Whose opinions should I seek? Pull yourself out of the tasks and ask yourself, "Is this really what we should be doing right now?"

In one of my very first leadership roles, I would constantly ask, "Why?" I was new and really wanted to understand the whys. The answer I would get was so often, "That's the way we've always done it." That's not really an answer, so I started to dig.

What I discovered was that the team I was on and now leading was given tasks to do without any responsibility for outcomes. There was a general lack of understanding between the goals and the tasks. Even the people who assigned us the tasks didn't truly understand why they were being assigned.

I started to investigate. I wouldn't be satisfied with the "that's the way we've always done it" reasoning. I would try to get to the bottom of it. And my efforts struck a nerve. Eventually, it became almost a cultural movement with my team and department. It wasn't just about finding why we did things, but it was also about aligning everyone to understand those reasons. It became a need for everyone to understand the value of the tasks.

Listen for Understanding

Up until now, we've talked about all the things you can do to become a strategic thinker. Now it's time to move to the ways you demonstrate that to those around you.

Listening is so critical on a leadership journey. It allows you to understand someone else's perspective. I had to learn to slow down to really hear people, to understand their perspective.

Listening is so critical on a leadership journey

There is so much misalignment on teams that comes from a lack of true listening. It can be very costly in an organization.

Slowing down and listening better actually improves alignment. Sometimes, listening is really hard. Too often, we listen for right or wrong. We listen to defend our perspective.

I challenge you to try true listening instead. The point is not to come to an agreement as you listen but rather for an understanding. Listen to see the issues and opportunities beyond your single perspective. If you struggle to get started, try asking a clarifying question such as "Tell me more" or "I haven't thought about it that way. Expand on that."

I mentioned "already listening" earlier. This isn't my phrase. I don't know where it came from, but my team started using that phrase to call each other out when we lost focus. We defined it as "I already know what you're going to say, so I stopped listening and am now crafting my response." Already listening does not give your speaker enough credit. It's a surefire way to be disrespectful of those around you.

Teams consist of both fast thinkers and processors. The fast thinkers are quickly ready to respond. Processors usually use a little more think time before responding. If you are a fast thinker, give processors that time. Slow down and really hear what others are saying. And if you're a processor, you still need to bring your thoughts forward, even if you feel they're not complete.

Already listening is a horrible habit. I have known about it for years and I still do it. There are times when a conversation starts to bore me and I'm ready to move on, but I know that about myself. I am challenging you as a strategic thinker (and myself as well) to listen for understanding. I can't reiterate this enough, especially in today's world.

Slow Down to Focus

Remember my most important message from the last chapter. Being clear and getting to the point is critical to be heard. When you slow your words, you become more intentional in the way you communicate. This is important as you clarify your message.

There's a component of busyness that also erodes our ability to demonstrate strategic thinking. Busyness looks like a lack of priorities, like everything is important, and therefore nothing is important. You can picture the busy female executive with stacks of papers and binders and a laptop. She's going back-to-back, meeting to meeting, walking fast and talking loud. Busy is not productive. Productivity has focus, it has intention, it has priorities.

If busy sounds like you, start by controlling your calendar. Give yourself time to process where you just came from and prepare to switch to where you're going. I was this person, right? I was the one who had my calendar packed. I had my notebook and I went from meeting to meeting, walking faster than I should in my shoes, making all this noise as I came in two minutes late while I was still trying to finish up a thought from a previous meeting. I was not doing justice to myself or my team.

Compare this picture to a senior executive who walks intentionally into a room a couple minutes early with nothing but the appropriate information. This executive knows the premeeting is important and is eager for it. This is the moment where relationships are built through informal conversations. This is where you get to know the people you work with. This is something that I miss when meetings and gatherings move virtual. It's harder to have informal conversations, to ask how things are outside the agenda. The senior executive knows the purpose of the meeting and is focused on the topic at hand, not trying to send off last-minute texts or emails before the conversation starts.

Which executive exudes confidence? Which one is ready for strategic discussions?

Warren Buffet said, "Busy is the new stupid." We wear our busyness as a badge of honor. When people ask, "How are you doing?" we respond, "I'm so busy." A thoughtful leader is busy but is also intentional, which doesn't exude busyness.

The client I mentioned earlier in this chapter who kept getting passed over was a classic doer. She was a high performer and really knew her stuff. People came to her to get things done. At meetings, she took most of the action items because she could get it done sooner and better. If you were to describe her in one word, it would be hyperbusy.

So she started working on that busyness. She took time before she said yes—again, intentional processing and thinking. That was the first step. She couldn't possibly be inquisitive or listen if her day was so completely full. She was able to churn out a lot of work. People knew she had high quality work and it was delivered on time, but that was part of the reason she wasn't perceived as a strategic thinker. Speed is very often perceived as counter to strategy.

This slowing down created a dilemma for her. She had to grapple with the fear that she wasn't being productive because she wasn't "doing." She had to transition and elevate her thinking. Solving problems with greater thought was actually solving them better. After grappling with this for a while, she has been able to let go and embrace that her new pace gives her the ability to think clearly and rationally, to understand the logical connections of the greater whole. She's a wonderful strategic thinker today.

Of course, she falls back on her competencies, but when she

needs to pull problems together or think about problems in a new way, she can actually facilitate that better than anybody I've seen. She is now a vice president of a large organization and is going to continue to move her career forward.

How can we see around the corner if we don't stop long enough to see the corner itself? To be a strategic thinker, you need to be both a doer and thinker. There are certainly urgent times when things need an immediate response, and that's when we need the doer. And there are times we need to pause and really question why we're going to space in the first place.

Having It ALL:
Actionable Leadership Lessons

Strategic thinking is about being a doer and a thinker. It is the ability to see around the corner. The way to do this is to think clearly and rationally as you seek to understand the logical connections between ideas, challenges, processes, and departments. It means slowing down and discovering what you don't know by listening for understanding.

Suggested Actions:

- Think about one specific task that is your responsibility. Who do you depend on to get this task complete? Who depends on you to complete the task? Have a conversation with everyone along the chain to understand the broader outcome or result. Then collaborate with your colleagues to find opportunities for improvements. Be curious.

- Recognize a coworker that you have difficulty with. In the next conversation with them, intentionally listen for understanding and ask clarifying questions such as "Tell me more" or "Can you expand on that?" Record the experience in your thought journal.

- When you find yourself in a diverging or brainstorming moment, try asking twice as many questions as solutions. Record the experience in your thought journal.

Download the free journaling worksheets or purchase the reflection guide workbook at **www.vickiupdike.com/ navigatingyourjourney.**

CHAPTER SIX

Create Your Executive Presence

Making an impact is directly connected to the executive presence you exude. The phrase "executive presence" is notoriously hard to define because there are so many different definitions. It's about a physical presence, sure. Stand up tall, sit up straight, pull your chair up to the table, and hold your space. But it goes beyond that.

I like to define it around an individual's confidence, credibility, and their ability to relate to others. It brings everything together that I have mentioned in this book so far.

This is a somewhat nebulous definition, and that's OK. Once you've seen it, you know what it is. Some people just have it. It's in the way they carry themselves. The way they can hold a room. When they speak, people listen. When others speak, they listen. In the beginning of the book, I mentioned the VP at my first job who made such an impact on me. She had an awesome executive presence. It was in her calmness, her clarity, and her authenticity. She told it like it was, which I still, to this day, reflect on and try to emulate as best I can.

I noticed she carried herself exactly the same way when interacting with everyone. She was able to do this as a leader within her peer group, with her team, and even with the president of the company. That was very natural to her. It's not like she turned on one channel for one group of people and another channel for a different group. She definitely had an impact.

The consistency of my VP was another thing I recognized in her. There are those people who take on a different posture when their boss walks into the room, for example. She had none of that. It didn't matter what environment she was in or who she was with, she was authentically herself all the time.

Her clarity and calmness gave people confidence in what she was saying and in her message. She had an impact no matter where she was. At times, the topic was hard and the decision was big. Where some leaders got visibly stressed, she would slow down and reflect even more on what was being told to her. She took time to process things and slowed down to carefully choose her words.

And then, of course, we've all seen that extremely competent colleague totally miss the mark on executive presence. They know their stuff, but, somehow, they come across confused and unorganized. Their words don't have confidence and clarity.

I worked with a leader who was an extreme example of this. I have looked back at this experience and tried to figure out just what it was about her that took away from her executive presence. The first word that comes to mind was "frazzled." She had an unorganized presence and thought process. It felt like she lacked focus and that her priorities were always someplace else when she was talking to me or anyone else. She was smart, no doubt, but it always felt like she was thinking about something else. This distraction exuded from her and didn't give us confidence in her leadership ability.

I was an individual contributor analyst with the company. There was a time when she was so disheveled as I was trying to talk to her about a very specific issue. I was standing in the doorway of her office to try to help her with a problem when she said, "Vicki, we need to talk about this, but let's go get a cappuccino and talk about it there."

Taking her lead, we drove a few miles to a local coffee shop. Once we were there, we sat for over an hour, and we didn't get anything done in all that time. We talked about all the things on her plate, random fires to be put out, but we never came back to that one issue that I was trying to address while standing in her doorway. I was happy to talk to her and hopefully help, but I continued to wonder at what point we would discuss the matter we had come to talk about. We never did.

I think she meant well to suggest getting off-site. Finding a fresh location can be very effective when you need to work through issues, but that's not what we did. As I look back, she walked in a rush, she talked in a rush, and she seemed to have three things going through her brain at the same time. It was all think-speak; whatever came to her mind, she spoke it. I kept wondering, *When are we going to stop talking about everything randomly and actually get something done?* There was little clarity. There was no calmness. It was unproductive, to say the least. She had very little executive presence.

Later on, I worked with a leader who also lacked that executive presence, but in an entirely different way. You've probably seen how some people really look the part, but they don't fit it. This coworker wore the expensive suits. He wore the expensive watch. He carried himself in that cool, calm, and collected way. He walked around the office with a swagger.

But he didn't authentically connect with us or the business issues we were working on. I didn't understand his priorities or his thinking. Part of having an executive presence is having influence by being heard and hearing others. I didn't get any of that from him. He might have been smart, but we would never know it. He was one of those people who used vague business words, the business-speak. You know what I'm talking about: "Based on quarterly benchmarks and capital functionalities, we will have to scale in our plan to dramatically, proactively aggregate process improvements ..."

He used a lot of those words that, together, have little meaning. Everybody's sitting around the table nodding. But when you dug a little deeper, it was hard to see if he had a meaningful point at all. There was no impression of competence behind it.

A part of executive presence is as simple as having the outside and the inside match. It's about having competence and sharing it effectively with others. You know your value and the technical skills that you have. This allows you to exude your confidence. You bring it together with clarity in a way that helps you influence people in a positive way.

Bringing It All Together

Executive presence is not about a title or an expensive suit. Looking the part is important, but it's not all about what you wear. It's not about clothes and jewelry and pulling your hair up in a bun. That may have been important at one time, but it's so much more than that. Executive presence is about stature and confidence wherever you are in your leadership journey. It's particularly important early on in your career.

It's about your stature, your confidence, your calmness, and the atmosphere you have around you. It is holding your head high, pulling your chair up to the table, and speaking with clarity. There's always an appropriateness, but don't let executive presence steal your uniqueness. You can spend hours researching what an executive is supposed to look like, but if the cake is only icing, you're missing the most important part.

Executive presence is about stature and confidence wherever you are in your leadership journey.

Your uniqueness should shine through your executive presence. Don't lose that. When you are uniquely you and when you master clear communication, you can have a powerful impact on people. You don't have to be an executive to have executive presence or to work on the skill of creating your executive presence.

One of the most important components of having an executive presence is in the influence you have on others. It works off a basic principle of trust. I can't feel trust toward anyone else until I feel trust toward myself. When you're confident in yourself, people feel they can have confidence in you, which builds trusting relationships. And building those trusting relationships are a key to having positive influence. The trust your team members have in you is a sign that you are well on your way to developing an executive presence.

Remember, you can't do this by yourself. Whether you're a member or a leader of a team, have that trust in others and in yourself. When you speak, people are going to listen because they know you understand. You will not downplay the people around you because your goal is to uplift everyone around you. They will be able to trust that you will be there to help them when they need you.

Instilling Confidence Through Uncertainty

I had a unique opportunity to work with many high-level women executives during the COVID-19 pandemic. When 2020 ended, I had a heart-to-heart with my coaching clients and asked them, "What have you learned this year?"

I knew that for every single one of them, the year had been so hard. Some didn't know if their company was even going to make it. It was a universally uncertain time for everyone. But it also showed us what we could do in extreme situations. It doesn't matter if the uncertainty is a pandemic or that your business is in trouble or there is an issue you can't solve. Those who have a true executive presence rise above uncertainty.

The thing that I heard from every single one of my clients was that they had an increase in confidence and an increase in their ability to follow their intuition to make decisions. They did it in their own unique ways, but when the issues got big, their executive presence manifested in greater clarity, confidence, and communication.

These presidents and business owners leaned into their intuition and their experience and had to make decisions fast. And that actually gave them greater confidence. There were times they couldn't stop and consider every possible outcome before making a decision. They had to grapple with questions like "Are we shutting the office down Monday?" and "Can I pay my employees this month?"

They learned that not every decision had to be a forever decision. If something went wrong, they had the ability to change it, which reduced that fear because things moved faster than they had anticipated. Yet they could adjust. They felt comfortable saying, "All right, did it work? If not, we're going to try something else." They discovered they could be flexible while still remaining confident.

Uncertain times are not the time to lose your executive presence. It is not the time to get frazzled. It is the time to slow down, create clarity, instill calmness, and embrace the influence you have.

As always, I told them (and most of my clients), "You are amazing. I wish you could see what I see."

Through uncertain times, your confidence will grow. It feels daunting when you're going through it, but looking back through those hardships, you will see how your executive presence moved you through more successfully.

Asking Is Another Form of Listening

Not just in uncertain times, listening is absolutely critical at all times. It is something we don't work on enough, but we all know we need to. Imagine what our society would be like if we all understood this one fundamental skill. But in reality, so few do.

We all know we need to be better listeners. Not listening for right or wrong. Not listening until I can give my next comment. Truly listening for understanding.

Having an executive presence is listening for understanding, valuing others' opinions and perspectives and the ability to seek out those opinions and perspectives from those around you, exuding the strategic thinking we mentioned in the prior chapter.

We all know what it feels like if we're not heard. One awesome way to show others that you are listening without always saying "I hear you" is to ask questions. That brings validity to their point. It builds that trust. The speaker will think, *She wants to hear more!*

I know there are times when we are like, *Okay, we already know that* or *This is ridiculous.* We all go through those moments in our heads. Instead of giving in to your head, though, go back and say, "Tell me more." Really. Because that ridiculousness may actually be a really creative point and your lack of listening for understanding is getting in your way.

There was a time in my career when I was accountable for sales. There comes a lot of pressure when that sales line is not running the way it should. One of the pressures is in operations because if sales are not hitting expectations, operations need to slow down. And when they slow down, they're not as efficient.

I kept getting this message from our operations team. They kept pushing my department to get more sales because operations were not as efficient as they could be. I got frustrated every time I heard this because it wasn't like we weren't trying to get sales in the door. Sales growth was our number one priority.

At one executive meeting, I had enough. In frustration, I snapped, "You know that you can batch the work in a way that makes you 100 percent efficient. Just do that!"

He could have blown my comment off as just an exasperated complaint, which it was. But instead, he listened for understanding. After the meeting, he went back and thought about my flip comment. A short time later, he came to me with an idea to close the facility on Wednesdays. To drive 100 percent efficiency, workers would put in four ten-hour days instead of the five eight-hour days. He wanted to make sure it didn't ruin our customer experience, so he came back to me.

We examined the idea and couldn't find anything wrong with it. I was shocked. Shocked that he listened to my ridiculousness. He had that executive presence. He was the one who slowed down and truly listened to my craziness. He presented the idea at the next meeting, and the plan went into effect. To this day, they still use that model when things slow down seasonally. He and I have both been long gone from that company, but the principle still works.

I'm not saying that being ridiculous is the best way to come up with ideas, but it's a great example of someone listening for the intent to understand and how it made a positive impact.

I believe in asking questions because so many times you DO know the answer, and we want to give you that answer. But this doesn't help those around you. When people come to us with questions or with issues, we perceive it as our problem to solve. We so willingly want to take the problem and solve it. That's in our nature.

Instead of taking the problem and solving it, ask questions so the person coming to you can also solve the problem. The importance of asking questions is not just for clarity for you, but sometimes it's for others to get clarity on their own points. This is a big part of having an executive presence, trusting in those around you to solve the problem. I don't need to take it away from you.

In my career, I valued being dependable. I got stuff done, right? I told you that in the beginning. But getting stuff done does not mean taking *all* the stuff. As you grow your career and build this executive presence, you learn that as you work through questions with others. The answer is often stronger than one person's perspective.

Take the Meaningful Components of Feedback

This is a big one.

I was a senior executive at a company and was still going through these moments where I bulldozed through conversations. As I've said, old habits die hard. I had a coach who was working me, helping me work through those moments. I knew I needed to figure out what I was doing, but I didn't know what I was doing.

One day, I was in a meeting with a few other executives who were all peers of mine. I don't even remember the topic that we were talking about, but I do remember it didn't go well. I was being bold. I was making my point. I was doing everything that I thought was right, but others just shut down. The meeting ended, and it just didn't feel right. I couldn't understand it.

I had learned by then that in these moments, I needed to go figure out why things went wrong because I couldn't see my blind spots. We all have blind spots in how we influence others.

I found this was a perfect opportunity to walk into my trusted colleague's office, right outside the meeting. I followed her into her office and shut the door. Because we had a very good relationship and had always been able to talk straight with each other, I knew I could ask her my question.

I simply asked, "Can you give me some feedback? What happened in there?"

Although simple words, these are the hardest words to say. It is an extremely vulnerable situation.

There was this awkward silence.

I know I had just opened a time for her to share something that she had never shared with me. She told me that I was jumping to conclusions too fast, and it felt like I was not really paying attention to other people's points.

I said, "Thank you" and left.

I felt like crap as I walked out of there. I wanted to be seen as a team player. I thought I had the trust and respect of my peer group, yet I just exuded the opposite things of all those things in a meeting. I didn't want to be seen that way, and yet that's what I was doing. It was hard to hear the feedback, and yet it was invaluable because it showed me a perfect example of when I do it wrong.

I reflected on her points and realized that I was uncomfortable with conflict. I realized I needed to allow time for others to debate points longer. I thought I already knew the problem and, as always, I was ready to solve it. But conflict is nothing more than different opinions about the same thing. Conflict is not fighting. It's not right or wrong. It's just understanding things from a different perspective. It was valuable for my team to have space to work through things.

Yet I was shutting it down and not allowing that conversation to happen. I perceived it as fighting, and I wanted everyone to get along. But the team wanted to have that healthy debate. In the meantime, I was looking like a know-it-all.

Knowing this blind spot allowed me to intentionally work on letting the debates and discussions continue. It's still uncomfortable for me, but I now see the value.

When you don't understand a blind spot of yours, asking for feedback is the best way to clarify. It's important to put yourself in that position to learn and grow. Feedback is often uncomfortable, so talk to someone you trust and whose opinions you value. Find a person who understands the situation differently than you do.

There are five steps to asking for feedback.

1. Set the tone. Tell your trusted person that you are coming to them to ask for feedback. When you explain that that's what you're doing, it sets the tone and brings down the defensive posturing. It allows the other person to see you in a more vulnerable light, and it puts the context of the conversation in place.

2. Ask the specific question that is unknown to you. In my case, I said, "Can you tell me what just happened in there?"

3. Listen. If you need to ask a clarifying question, that's OK, but keep that very limited.

4. Thank them for the feedback. The sooner you can get to this part, the better it is. Watch out for feelings of defensiveness. If you get your hackles up in the slightest, then the person giving you the feedback will be less honest the next time because they will know you really don't want to hear honesty. The point is for you just to hear the perspective and then say, "Thank you."

5. Reflect on what the feedback means for you. How do you want to change your behavior?

Asking for feedback is a really great way to start building trust, but it's humbling and it's hard. As I was writing out this story, I could still feel the tension in my stomach. Of course, not all feedback is good. There are times when you may decide to not take the feedback, and that's still your quiet decision, but continue to seek and value feedback.

Be gracious and accept whatever is offered. After all, nobody has to tell you anything. Honesty is a gift that we should always be grateful for.

Having It ALL:
Actionable Leadership Lessons

Everything in this book has been leading up to executive presence. If you walk away and only remember one thing, let it be this: leadership is about your executive presence. And executive presence is about having confidence, clarity, vision, humility, curiosity, poise, and good judgment.

When you focus on building your executive presence, you almost can't help but have a greater influence on those around you. And that is the whole point of taking the leadership journey in the first place, right?

Suggested Actions:

- Make a list of the most influential people you know in person. They can be past teachers, coaches, relatives, managers, and fellow employees.

- Once you are done, look at that list as a whole and try to pick out commonalities that these people have. Chances are, if they were influential on you, they were probably influential on others, which means they must have had at least some executive presence. Which of the traits you've learned about so far can you identify in them?

- During your next difficult conversation, practice active listening. Truly listen for understanding vs. already listening. In your thought journal, record the details of that conversation privately. When you know you are going to report on something, you listen differently.

- Feedback is critical to your leadership development. Identify someone you trust and ask them for feedback the next time you sense contention or conflict or just that you don't have the whole picture. Use the feedback form from the workbook or my website.

Download the free journaling worksheets or purchase the reflection guide workbook at **www.vickiupdike.com/ navigatingyourjourney**.

CHAPTER SEVEN

Creating Balance: Our Superpower

I t always amazes me to see how women find creative ways to have it all. No matter what challenges come, we have the capacity to always find a way to do what we love, whether it be taking care of children, spending time with friends, or leading a company. This is our superpower.

But so often, we doubt this in ourselves. We get stuck in certain ways of thinking that hold us back. Particularly for women who are mothers.

I was giving a keynote for the Girl Scout Association. In the audience were mothers and young women in high school and college. The theme of the night was the balance of motherhood, all the things moms have to do to manage it all, and how to instill competence in our young girls at the same time. That is a heavy task.

I was on a panel that discussed strategies and tactics to address these balance challenges. The discussion touched on feelings of guilt, overwhelm, and regret that so many mothers feel.

Nearing the end of this discussion, a young woman who had been sitting in the back raised her hand. She stood up and said, "You know, I've been listening to this for the last hour. I am working through college, and I want you to know that as a daughter, I am kind of confused about what you are all talking about. As I was growing up, I didn't feel any of this. From what I can see, you are doing great."

Thinking about this still gives me chills. I thanked her for standing up and saying that because most of the women in the room needed to hear her perspective. She did not recognize or feel the stress that we were all certain our children were absorbing. It made everyone feel tremendously relieved to know that here was a young girl, whose mother was probably close in age to many of those in the audience, and she was fine. She was evidence that there was no reason for our guilt.

Challenge of Balance

No matter if they are mothers or not, many women struggle with balance. Everybody tells us we should have balance, but what does that mean?

Balance can only be defined by the individual. If you work sixty hours a week and life is balanced for you, don't feel bad that you're working sixty hours a week. That is your balance. If you can work twelve because your life is filled with other worthy causes, that is your balance.

Balance can only be defined by the individual

There was a young woman who worked in my office, and when I left every night, she was still there. She would work late, which kind of made me feel bad. Every night, I told her to go home as I was walking out the door at 5:30 p.m. But that wasn't her balance. She wanted those hours late at night. Her life worked for her. Me imposing my balance on her was completely inappropriate. If that was where she found her productive time, that was just fine! Who was I to judge? Incidentally, she is now a fine executive out in Colorado and living her best life.

Now, there are a ton of things that get in our way of balance. One big one is that we put far too much pressure on ourselves to be the best at everything. We want to be the best friend, the best daughter, the best mother, the best professional, the best spouse or partner. We put this expectation on ourselves that comes from nowhere but inside ourselves.

I know you want to do well. And I know you want to exude that, but pressure to be the best in every category all the time is not healthy. There was no more obvious proof of this than during the COVID-19 pandemic. Nearly every day, there was another headline about how women were suffering more than men, particularly because we were challenging every aspect of our lives. We were challenged to be professionals because professional life transformed. We were challenged at being mothers because our kids' lives changed. We were challenged at being daughters because our parents were impacted. We felt like we were sucking at everything we did because we couldn't do it all. Of course, that is just one single example of how, when things in our world change, the stress of that change collapses on us. This idea of being perfect in all those spaces is unrealistic.

Another thing that gets in our way is always being "on." This is a beautiful, technological world we're living in, and I could not do without it. But I think you'd agree that technology is in our faces too much. We feel we have to have our phones on all the time. We have the alerts sounding. We have to check our email and our social channels. But then the user data reports pop up and reflect back on how you're not being perfect. It's so annoying. This can really get in your way of defining balance for your life. You don't have to be the person next to you. You don't have to be your coworker. Being "on" gives you too many things to compare yourself to and hijacks your ability to focus.

We also struggle to find balance when we give in to limiting beliefs. Some women feel they have to choose balance over a career. They think, *I can't be a manager because I really want a better work-life balance.* That is a limiting belief because there are ways to build a career path with balance. I have shared some of my own experiences finding my way through this in prior chapters. If balance means working twenty hours a week, that's yours to define. If it means working sixty, that's yours too. I believe you can have it all, whatever all is for you.

For me personally, keeping my personal life separate from my work life was adding stress to my balance. I discovered that when I show everybody the whole picture of me, it actually starts defining and justifying balance to those around me. I already mentioned in previous chapters how I had tried to keep my personal life away from my work life. But it was vice versa as well.

People in my personal life didn't even realize what I was doing in my work life. How do you explain to a kid a complex concept like marketing? I was at my first company when my daughter was little, so I never really took the time to try to explain it. She kind of understood that what I did had something to do with the catalogs that she saw in the mail. So in her little mind, she literally thought I wrote addresses on envelopes. That was cute.

My grown family members barely knew what I did either. There was a time when my mom and aunt came to one of my keynote speeches. They were just so cute there sitting in the back. They just wanted to be there to see what I do and support me.

I was up there speaking on the topics that I have experience in and they were sitting in the back being entertained.

Shortly after it was over, I overheard my mother talking to my sister. My sister asked her, "So what was it like?"

My mother said, "Well, it sounded like Vicki, but I had no idea who she was!"

Of course, my family knew what I did, but I never had said anything like "I'm the president of the company. I have to deal with cashflow, and there are a lot of zeros I have to keep track of. And I make important decisions for thousands of people that I have working at the company. That's what I do every day."

Nope. To them, I'm just Vicki. I never needed any accolades for the milestones I had in my career. But it was a little sad that they didn't know that part of me. If you come home and don't share that work with your personal life, that adds stress to the balance. Once I started really bringing those together, that's when keeping that balance became a bit easier.

Clarify Your Boundaries

Let's define the word "boundary." Merriam-Webster's Dictionary states a boundary is "something that indicates or fixes a limit or extent." That doesn't sound good to me. Alternately, the *Oxford English Diction- ary* defines it as "a line that marks the limits of an area, a dividing line." That better reflects what we are talking about here. They're both definitions of a boundary, right? But when you're talking about the challenges women face with boundaries and life balance, it is a line that marks your limit.

But how do you find your limit? That is one of the hardest things to personally define.

Start by taking a step back and asking yourself, "What is causing me stress?" When you're in those moments of stress, reflect on the circumstances. What are you doing and who are you engaging with?

Ask yourself what's going on and then pay attention to the emotions you're feeling. These are the boundary moments. Are you feeling angry or sad or resentful, or are you feeling energized and satisfied? These emotions can be a good sign that a boundary is being crossed for you. When you identify what side you're on, that really is an indication where your boundary lines are.

Once you recognize there is a line, the next step is to consider your priorities. We all know we should have priorities. I know you probably could list your top five right off the bat. But what I'm talking about is so much harder than just rattling off a list because each of those things is important. They all allow you to live the life that you're living. You need them all. Just not all at the same time.

It's OK that priorities change over time. They may even change day to day. For me, my children were my number one priority. Period. I built a wonderful career, but I was raising those kids, and my focus was to have them raised as productive adult humans. That was so important.

But there were times when I needed to leave town in my career. I tried to keep it to a two-night minimum, but of course, sometimes with business, that's not possible. So the priority in those few days when I was traveling was the work I was doing. I was able to shed everything else and put that as my priority for that time. If I didn't do well in my work life in those trips, it wouldn't matter to my children. I was still gone from home. I set them up so they knew where I was going and for how long. They knew I was only going to be gone for a few days, and that my work was going to be a priority for that time.

I was able to make the trip my priority and know that things at home were taken care of. We didn't have video chat back then. We barely had texting. But that was a good thing, actually. I found the more we talked on the phone to each other, the more my stress increased. My kids knew that Mom was unavailable for the next two days and couldn't wait to see them Wednesday. I set that boundary for myself and for them.

Of course, they knew they could always reach me, but it had to be pretty important. I knew when I got a call from home when I was traveling that it must be kind of serious or important. Once, at a business dinner, my phone vibrated, and my home number popped up on the screen. My first instinct was, "Oh no!"

I asked to be excused. My son was on and said, "Mom, I got an A!" He was so proud. I took the moment to celebrate the A, felt that tug of wishing I was there, and went back to work. These are some of the challenges we face.

When you're looking at your priorities, ask yourself what you are willing to sacrifice. And for how long? For me, I was willing to say to the kids, "Are you good for two days?" They were, so it wasn't a big sacrifice to shift that priority for short periods of time.

Reprioritizing also means asking yourself, "Is this really necessary?"

That's a hard question to ask because we want to be perfect in everything. But is it truly necessary? Another way to think of it is worst-case scenario. So what if you don't do that thing? So what if it doesn't get done? So what if it's not perfect?

> *Reprioritizing also means asking yourself, "Is this really necessary?"*

What's the worst that will happen? So often the impacts are less than what you are playing out in your head.

Once you have answered these questions, write down your answers. What are your month's priorities? What are your week's priorities, and how does that trickle down to you today? How do your priorities need to shift right now?

If it's baseball season and you're at your son's game every night, that is the priority for this season. Work around it. But then when it's budgeting season and you're working till eight o'clock every night, that is the priority.

It's not changing your boundary. It is flexing the priorities within your boundaries.

Sometimes we feel like boundaries are too bold because we want to be the people pleaser. We want to say yes when we should say no. You have the audacity to protect your priorities and boundaries. When you do that, you protect your confidence and your space. When you don't have boundaries, you're not progressing as the leader. You are seen as someone that we just dump work on.

Don't be that person. It is within your control to take back your space and your priorities when other people try to take them over.

Boundaries in Unusual Circumstances

Unusual circumstances happen to everyone. That's the one thing we can pretty much count on. Things will go wrong sometimes, and we have to figure out what to do next.

An obvious example is the 2020 quarantine that happened as a result of the COVID-19 pandemic. So many women were faced with boundaries in ways they had never been before. Boundaries are necessary whether you work from home or in a busy office. Here are four suggestions that can help, no matter what circumstances we find ourselves working under.

1. Create clear start and end times to your workday. Before the pandemic, many of us enjoyed drive time to and from work, which gave us space to shift mental gears. In lieu of a commute, try establishing a small ritual to signal the start and end of your day. For example, begin each morning with coffee and a book, and wrap up each workday with a walk on the treadmill. These simple activities will create physical and mental bookends around your work schedule.

2. Unplug during nonwork hours. This requires you to first determine what those "nonwork hours" are. If you enjoy logging in to catch up on work late at night, that's fine. But do set aside certain hours as untouchable, for example, between 5:00 and 9:00 p.m. each day. Then spend those hours disconnected from phones and email and enjoy time with your family or pursuing nonwork activities.

3. Add self-care to your schedule. Repeat after me: self-care is not selfish. It's a necessary component in the life of a healthy, productive employee. If you burn out, you'll be no good to anyone—not your boss, your coworkers, your family, or yourself. So ensure you'll take care of yourself by scheduling self-care into your week and treating those appointments as nonnegotiable. Maybe for you that means a massage, a movie, or an hour sipping wine with a friend. Or it can be as simple as planning ahead for a nap or a walk around the neighborhood.

4. Build a community. Finally, remember as human beings we were made to crave relationships. Although we may not be sharing space with our colleagues at the moment, we can still build a community of like-minded people to support and encourage us. Women's Leadership Academy is here to help you feel part of something bigger—a group of women navigating their career ambitions together, building off of each other's experiences to gain confidence and feel part of a community.

By creating healthy boundaries, caring for yourself, and connecting with peers outside of work, you can thrive in today's challenging environment and continue growing toward your goals.

Communicating Your Boundaries

How do you show others your boundaries? First, you have to know where they are. Next, when a decision is presented to you that you suspect might come up against a boundary, take your time to respond. Do not say yes immediately. That thoughtfulness and reflection is extremely important. If you say yes too quickly, your boundaries will disintegrate.

I coach a wonderful woman who would always take the problems of those who came to her because she liked being a resource. She felt there was value by taking on more. But that behavior was not falling in her priorities. She had to change her mindset that leadership isn't about taking the issue on herself. It's about helping the person through the issue. It's about letting the issue or the challenge or the work stay with the person coming to you with it. That is holding your line and saying "No." There's an old but wise saying: when you say no to others, you say yes to yourself.

Others need to know your boundaries. I had a boss who had a habit of texting in the middle of the night. He was a great guy and certainly didn't mean any harm by it. That was just when he did his thinking. He never expected a response.

But what he didn't realize was that I had teenage kids and I never turned my ringer off. When my phone would go off in the middle of the night, that was every mom's nightmare. I had to tell him that he had to stop because I could not handle the stress of my phone going off in the middle of the night. He was fine with it. He just timed the messages to go out in the morning. It was my way of knowing my boundaries and communicating them with others before I grew resentful.

Another way I communicated my boundaries was by putting my kids' sporting events in my work calendar. Without saying anything, I clearly communicated the priority. It was a priority for me to be there, so the people I worked with respected that.

There are always exceptions, but you should not compromise a boundary unless it is truly an exception, the-ship-is-burning kind of stuff.

Too many women aren't taught boundaries. Identify what's causing you stress and reflect on that. Then pull yourself out of it and look for the root cause. It's not that I just have to get the budget done this month, for example. Ladder that up. I'm working ten-hour days. Ladder up again. I'm working so much because I'm not delegating well enough. Or maybe I am taking on too much at home at the time when I know I have big projects at work. Most often, you'll find the causes are within your control. That's where boundaries come in.

Once you figure out where boundaries need to be, women often have a sense of fear to institute them. If I have a boundary, I feel like I might lose a client, lose a friend, or get demoted. Or I'm not going to be seen as ready for the next step. How do you exude those boundaries and get your work done?

I want you to go back to your value and your competence. Reread those chapters and remind yourself that you are worth advocating for. You have to understand the value you bring to the organization and the competence that you need to observe to own your boundaries. A boundary may take a conversation with your boss: I need to leave at 4:30 p.m. to see my son's baseball game once a week. Don't ask for permission. It's your boundary and you own it. Nobody else can tell you what your boundary is. Just inform them and then ask how they can help you work around that. Those hard conversations come back to your confidence level because they don't come naturally to us.

This is not sacrificing the components of doing your job. It is only going to earn you respect.

Give Yourself a Break

On Mother's Day 2021, I wrote a blog post for my website (newsagestrategies.com) and shared it with all of my clients. I was surprised and amazed at the massive positive response that followed. Clearly, no matter how often we hear this message, we need to hear it again. And again. I don't think women can be reminded too often that they deserve a break.

This is what the blog post said:

Conflicting priorities are a given; guilt is not.

My family, including my two grown kids (twenty-one and twenty-four), was having a good talk over a recent holiday break. I'm not really sure how we got on the topic, but I started to mention the things I missed when they were little and I was working full time. This included things such as my daughter's first day of kindergarten because of a missed airport connection, my son's eighth grade graduation—simply because I forgot to put it on my calendar—the nights I was late for dinner, and our rushed mornings just to get out the door. As I spoke, they couldn't even remember these things. I have been carrying this guilt with me for all these years, and they don't even remember! How is it that I burdened myself all this time, and for no reason? Since that time, I've significantly reshaped my perspective on mom guilt, and I hope these ideas will help other women.

Give yourself a break. Every person, no matter his or her vocation, will face conflicting priorities. It's natural to have to make choices, shift schedules, or even check out for some self-care. Conflicting priorities in life are a given, but feeling guilty about them is not. In the midst of overlapping obligations, make your choice and then commit to being 100 percent present. You will reinvigorate your thoughts and actions with a renewed sense of purpose.

Create family time. Hire a cleaning service, get someone to mow your lawn, or arrange for someone to drive your kids to school. There is no guilt in these decisions because you are aligning your choices with your priorities—which likely include proper rest and more good times spent with friends and loved ones.

Set expectations and communicate them to people at work and at home. For example, my kids knew that when I traveled, I would not be immediately reachable 100 percent of the time. They understood that Wednesdays were my nights to work late, so they weren't anxious if I wasn't home for dinner. There is freedom in setting routines that honor you and the people who depend on you.

Don't make perfection your goal. Much of what you see on social media are the highlight reels of your friends' lives—which means all the everyday messy and mundane parts are on the cutting room floor. Like my kids told me, some of those clips are completely forgotten, and there is real grace in that.

My daughter says some of the warmest memories of her young childhood were the quiet times we spent together reading or talking or watching TV before her bedtime. In feeling guilty about the events I missed, I had assigned value to certain experiences and wrongly assumed my young children felt the same way too. As it turns out, I am a pretty good mom, and I'm sure you are too. And it doesn't require one bit of guilt to get us there.

We feel that missing the first day of kindergarten or a basketball game will have major long-term effects on our kids. But in the end, they most appreciated the quiet times when we are just with them. For me, that quiet time was the last hour of the day. My son and daughter and I would have dinner and then goof around, watch shows, and eat Cheez-Its. That was our time together.

Each evening, we would sit together for dinner and talk about our day. I always found that the yes/no questions never led to good conversation. I knew they wanted to talk, so instead of just asking, "Did you have a good day?" I would say, "Tell me about the best part of your day."

I remember so clearly once when my daughter said, "I think it's coming. I think it's tonight." She said that because she was looking forward to that quiet time we always had at the end of the day. That's how much those simple moments of just being together meant to her.

Even though my children are grown and have moved into their adult lives (with success, I have to proudly add!), this memory is still so clear.

When we talk about boundaries, it can be just an hour at night where you turn everything off. Those are the lasting moments that matter. You work hard. It's OK if you don't make the perfect birthday party every year. Or be at every single basketball game. Protect the times that really matter.

When you are able to choose and enforce good boundaries, you will find this allows you to go much further than you ever thought you could. You will be able to achieve more than you expected. But sometimes boundaries have to be expanded, not narrowed. I learned this when I was just a teenager.

Aim High

In high school, I was a mediocre student. I was a middle child. I lived in a middle-class family in the Midwest. My life was middle every-thing. I had no intention of going to college after I graduated. But something happened that changed that, and with it, the course of my entire life. And it happened after a bike ride of all things.

When I was a senior in high school, I did a charity bike ride challenge with my family. I don't even know if it was ten miles or fifty miles, but it felt like a hundred miles because I was exhausted at the end. We all went to get lunch at a cute little diner to celebrate. I sat across from my uncle, who was the first person in my extended family to go to college. I had always really respected his opinion. While we were eating, he turned to me and said, "So, Vicki, what are you doing next year?"

I said, "I don't know. I think I might just get a job. I'm thinking maybe I'll be a secretary. I really like keeping things organized. Maybe I'll be a legal secretary."

I think I only said that because I thought it sounded more important. He looked right at me and said, "Vicki, why don't you be the lawyer?"

At that time, going to college wasn't on my horizon, much less something like law school. But his question was real—"why not?" It changed my perspective in a very casual conversation.

I just didn't see it. At this point, I was late to the game, but I applied to three schools and got into all three. I picked the one that I thought would be the best fit for me, and I ended up being the first woman in my full extended family to get a bachelor's degree and then a master's degree later in life.

To think back on that simple conversation in the diner and see the influence it had on me is amazing. I had no idea I wasn't aiming high enough. There was really no reason for it. I just didn't even give myself enough credit to aim higher. I could be the lawyer or the leader or the business owner.

I have sent my uncle many thank-you cards throughout my career. When I moved back to the area where my family lives in northeast Wisconsin and found a career that matched my skills and my future as the leader that I wanted to be, I sent him a thank-you card. When I paid off my student loans, I sent him a thank-you card. That simple conversation was a domino. It was that starting down a road that changed my life.

Never stop learning. Life changes over time. That's a given. The definition of your boundaries changes over time. Your priorities change. That's life; embrace it.

Learning and growing is never done. Learn in the way that makes sense for you. Is it reading? Is it networking with professionals you admire or with moms you admire? Is it listening to podcasts? Is it listening? Is it attending webinars?

How can you get out of your own perspective? Part of aiming high is being curious and intentional. It is having the attitude that you can learn from anyone. A senior executive I know found a young person in their early twenties and asked them to be a mentor. What a wonderful thing. Can you imagine what might happen if a board of directors took some time to earnestly learn from the young people in the company? I wouldn't be surprised if they achieved greater things together than they ever did before.

As you continue to learn and grow, your life and career is yours to evolve as well. If you don't have a wonderful uncle like mine, use your network. It will show you the examples of what is possible. Go to the networking events and talk to those you admire. Build that network, even inside your company.

I have a coaching client who is not an executive yet, but she has set a goal to become one. When she's invited to be in executive meetings, she feels so reluctant to speak. She feels like she is there just to be a listener. We talked about confidence and about the opportunity she has to show her skill and her value. Together, we set goals to help her in those situations to take her space, be heard, and exude the executive presence that is within her. Being silent doesn't take advantage of these opportunities. These are the moments where you can demonstrate your executive presence, but you have to actively engage.

By setting goals and aiming high, you are working toward something rather than working for the sake of working. Intentionally set a road map to get to those higher goals. It's for you to take control and own the next steps. Your journey can move toward something greater instead of waiting for something to happen.

By doing this, you're going to find where you need improvement. You're going to find the gaps. And most importantly, you will start closing the gaps. I had to go get an MBA, but in the end, that helped me gain motivation. No matter what goals you have, you are going to continue to gain motivation. You're going to find satisfaction in your career because you are going where you want to go.

In the beginning of my journey, I was scared. I had so many doubts. Likewise, you will have times when you'll wonder if it is worth it. You'll ask yourself if you are on the right journey at all. And that is OK. It's OK to have the ups and downs on the journey. That is normal and to be expected.

Don't lose sight of your goals and what it takes to get there. If you don't have that place where you want to go, how do you know you're ever going to get there? For me, it was going back to get my MBA and facing the burden of adding one more thing to my already busy, complicated life. In the end, it worked out. I had doubts. It was hard. But I did it. There was a sense of accomplishment that nobody can ever take away from me.

I am still setting goals and learning to this day. I can barely speak a story, let alone write one, and yet people want to hear my story. Here I am, writing this book. I never thought that was possible!

In the end, I have learned that the journey is everything. Learning what your *ALL* is can include heartache, joy, embarrassment, and pride. But that's the whole point. It's every little step we take in between the milestones that counts most.

Work through those less confident moments. Do it anyway. Don't let the little voice in your head hold you back. Aim high. Dream big. Create the balance. Draw the lines. You can do it!

You are entirely up to you.

Having It ALL:
Actionable Leadership Lessons

Now that you have a pretty good idea of what your "all" is and you have a plan on how to get there, don't jeopardize all your hard work by letting anything take that away. Demands from other people, bad habits, and self-defeating beliefs can all put you at risk of losing the path to it all. Keep your vision clear and your goals high.

Aiming high is more than just setting lofty goals. It is about having a lifetime learner attitude. It is about pushing yourself more than you would otherwise. But it is also about doing what is best for you. It may take your whole life to master, but I believe you will be able to have it "all"!

Suggested Actions:

- Recognize that stressful moments are often indicators of boundaries being crossed. Reflect on the causes of stress for you and consider what boundaries you need to clarify.

- Document your priorities and recognize that they can shift from month to month or even day to day. My guess is your top five priorities never change but the sequencing of them may. Writing them down can relieve the stress of having multiple priorities and help you see that they are not necessarily conflicting.

- Go back to your goal sheet from chapter two and rewrite new goals. It's been a journey. Aim high!

Download the free journaling worksheets or purchase the reflection guide workbook at **www.vickiupdike.com/ navigatingyourjourney.**

ABOUT THE AUTHOR

Vicki Updike is the president and founder of New Sage Strategies, a women's leadership development company equipping women with the tactics and strategies to continue to build their careers. Prior to consulting, Vicki's corporate leadership journey included various marketing and executive positions. Her last corporate position was president of Silver Star Brands.

Having been a president and C-suite executive gives Vicki unique perspective in coaching and business advising. She brings experience in the areas of strategic planning and execution, organizational development, and leadership coaching.

Vicki is passionate about helping create strong, effective leaders and leadership teams and is invested in the education, support, and encouragement of professional women. She loves a good challenge and leans on her knowledge and experiences to help build results-minded leadership qualities in each person or group she gets the privilege to work alongside.

She is a longtime resident of northeast Wisconsin, where she lives with her husband, Jim. She has two grown children, who are her greatest accomplishments. She is involved in the community and many nonprofit organizations.

To learn more about Vicki and navigating your journey, visit www.VickiUpdike.com.

CPSIA information can be obtained
at www.ICGtesting.com
Printed in the USA
JSHW022220191021
19689JS00007B/150